# *remembering*
# GOD'S MERCY

"Dawn Eden manages to flawlessly bring together Jesus, Mary, the apostles, Pope Francis, and St. Ignatius. It is an inspired work. Like Mary, I treasured up and pondered the insights."

**Rev. Mark E. Thibodeaux, S.J.**
Author of *Reimagining the Ignatian Examen*

"By showing how every memory can become a place of encounter with God, Dawn Eden gently reveals how we can be freed from the prison of our wounds, not by fleeing pain but by letting God turn it into gift. Compelling and direct, drawing honestly from her own painful memories, *Remembering God's Mercy* is a rich and sensitive meditation on Francis's 'Revolution of Tenderness.' Whether studied as theology, used as a companion on retreat, or read in quiet moments, it is a life-changing book."

**Austen Ivereigh**
Author of *The Great Reformer: Francis and the Making of a Radical Pope*

"This is an exceptional book. In her usual highly readable and storytelling style, Dawn Eden helps us understand the Ignatian spirituality of Pope Francis, as well as how and why suffering can be 'redemptive.' *Remembering God's Mercy* breaks new ground and adds significantly to works about healing from trauma and the painful memories that follow."

**Rev. James Kubicki, S.J.**
National Director of the Apostleship of Prayer

"Dawn Eden presents texts by three Jesuits—Ignatius of Loyola, Peter Faber, and Pope Francis—that show the importance they give to memory. This is a deeply thought-provoking Ignatian reflection on what pain, and even trauma, can teach us about our longing for healing, redemption, and resurrection."

**Rev. Hans Zollner, S.J.**
President of the Centre for Child Protection of the
Pontifical Gregorian University in Rome

# *remembering* GOD'S MERCY

## Redeem the Past and Free Yourself from Painful Memories

Dawn Eden

Ave Maria Press AVE Notre Dame, Indiana

In accordance with c. 827, permission to publish is granted on October 30, 2015, by Very Reverend Ronald A. Hicks, Vicar General of the Archdiocese of Chicago. Permission to publish is the official declaration of ecclesiastical authority that the material is free from doctrinal and moral error. No legal responsibility is assumed by the grant of this permission.

---

Founded in 1865, Ave Maria Press is a ministry of the United States Province of Holy Cross.

www.avemariapress.com

Paperback: ISBN-13 978-1-59471-636-2

E-book: ISBN-13 978-1-59471-637-9

Cover image © Srdjan Kirtic/Stocksy.

Cover design by Kristen Hornyak Bonelli.

Text design by Andy Wagoner.

Printed and bound in the United States of America.

*Library of Congress Cataloging-in-Publication Data*
Names: Eden, Dawn, 1968-
Title: Remembering God's mercy : redeem the past and free yourself from
   painful memories / Dawn Eden.
Description: Notre Dame : Ave Maria Press, 2016. | Includes bibliographical
   references.
Identifiers: LCCN 2015039366| ISBN 9781594716362 (pbk.) | ISBN
9781594716379
   (e-book)
Subjects: LCSH: God (Christianity)--Mercy. | Regret--Religious
   aspects--Christianity. | Spiritual life--Catholic Church. | Catholic
   Church--Doctrines.
Classification: LCC BT153.M4 E28 2016 | DDC 248.8/6--dc23
LC record available at http://lccn.loc.gov/2015039366

|||||||||||||||||||||||||||||||||||||||||||||||||||||||||||||||||||||||

# TO FR. LOUIS J. TWOMEY, S.J.
# (1905-1969)

who helped countless people, near and far,
pass over from a slave memory to a free one,
whose big heart drew its strength from
the Sacred Heart,
and who completed his life's Suscipe
murmuring with labored breaths,
"All for Thee,"
this book is lovingly dedicated.

# CONTENTS

||||||||||||||||||||||||||||||||||||||||||||||||||||||||||||||||||||

# PREFACE

I wrote this book to share the good news that Jesus
Christ heals our memories.

There has been a growing recognition in recent years
that those of us who suffer the effects of painful memories need more than just psychological help. Therapy can
help us cope, but if we are truly to break free from the
grip of past pain, we need *spiritual* help. Only the love
of God can untangle the web of regrets and resentments
that prevent us from moving forward. Only the Divine
Physician can heal our heart.

And heal it he does. The good news of Jesus' power
to renew us resonates throughout sacred scripture and
Christian tradition—if only we know where to look.

Scripture tells us, "God sent his only Son into the
world so that we might have life through him" (1 Jn
4:9)—that we might live in Christ's light, and not in
the shadows of past pain. The *Catechism* tells us, "The
Word became flesh so that thus we might know God's
love" (CCC 458). And Church Fathers such as Gregory
of Nazianzus tell us that the Word assumed a human
mind so that he might heal every human mind: "That

which was not assumed is not healed; but that which is united to God is saved."[1]

When Jesus was suffering on the Cross, he was given the opportunity to deaden his consciousness. Mark's gospel tells us that the soldiers offered him wine drugged with myrrh. "But he did not take it" (Mk 15:23).

Why did he refuse? Blessed John Henry Newman offers an intriguing answer. Jesus, Newman says, did not wish to limit his sufferings to the pain of the present moment. In other words, Jesus made a conscious choice to experience the pain of memory.

To explain this point, Newman first observes that, in our own human experience, we can tolerate almost any amount of pain if it lasts but a brief moment and is gone. The pain becomes intolerable only when it continues. That is why patients who are undergoing a medical procedure find themselves wishing they could stop the doctor's hand: they feel "they have borne as much as they can bear; as if the continuance and not the intenseness was what made it too much for them."[2]

And so it is, Newman says, that "the memory of the foregoing moments of pain acts upon and (as it were) edges the pain that succeeds."[3]

> If the third or fourth or twentieth moment of pain could be taken by itself, if the succession of the moments that preceded it could be forgotten, it would be no more than the first moment, as bearable as the first (taking away the shock which accompanies the first); but what makes it unbearable is, that it *is* the

> twentieth; that the first, the second, the third,
> on to the nineteenth moment of pain, are all
> concentrated in the twentieth; so that every
> additional moment of pain has all the force,
> the ever-increasing force, of all that has pre-
> ceded it.[4]

Jesus, therefore, refused the drugged wine because, knowing that his sufferings would save us, he was "bent on bearing the pain in all its bitterness."[5]

What I like about Newman's insight is that it does more than help us understand who Jesus was. It helps us understand who he is.

We already know from the witness of the Gospel that Jesus, having risen, retains the physical wounds he suffered upon the Cross (Jn 20:20, 27). Newman follows this to its logical implication: Jesus must then also retain his invisible wounds—the memories of each moment of his sufferings.

But how, you may ask, can Jesus retain his memories of pain, given that there are no tears in heaven (Rv 21:4)?

The answer, I believe, is that, just as in the Resurrection Jesus' visible wounds are now transfigured, radiating grace (Jn 1:14), so too his invisible wounds are now glorified. All Jesus' sufferings remain etched in his memory, but his memories of them no longer bring him feelings of pain. In his risen state, when he remembers his passion, he remembers only his *passion*—the overpowering love he bore that led him to shed every last drop of his Precious Blood for our salvation.

Wouldn't it be wonderful to "have the mind of Christ" (1 Cor 2:16)? To be able to look back at your entire life, both the joys and the sufferings, and to see only the love of God? That was my thought when I wrote *My Peace I Give You: Healing Sexual Wounds with the Help of the Saints*. In that book, I sought to help my fellow victims of childhood sexual abuse heal their memories through the lives of saints who, having suffered trauma, found healing in Christ.

The response to *My Peace I Give You* was unlike anything I have experienced as a writer. Every author wants her book to be appreciated by its intended audience, and mine certainly was; readers who were survivors of abuse told me it helped them where other books had not. What was unusual was that, again and again, even as readers thanked me for *My Peace I Give You*, they asked me to give them something more. They wanted me to write a new book—one that would present the same healing spirituality, but in a way that they could share it with loved ones who had not suffered abuse.

It touched me that my readers wanted me to make the message of *My Peace I Give You* accessible to a wider audience, and I hoped to fulfill their desire. There was just one problem: inspiration. If I was to revisit the topic of healing of memories, I would need a fresh angle, a new source of wisdom from which to draw.

I found that source of wisdom in Pope Francis. On March 30, 2013, just seventeen days after his election, the Holy Father gave an Easter Vigil homily in which he spoke of how the risen Christ leads us to heal our memories (see chapter 3). In an interview later that year, when asked about his manner of prayer, Francis spoke of how the Spiritual Exercises of St. Ignatius of Loyola—which were part of his training as a Jesuit—had helped him develop "a prayer full of memory" (see chapter 6).[6]

Francis's comments about the Spiritual Exercises especially intrigued me, because he referred to an exercise that I used as the basis of the spirituality of *My Peace I Give You*: the Contemplation to Attain the Love of God, which includes St. Ignatius's best-known prayer, the Suscipe. His observations on that exercise confirmed my previous intuition regarding the value of Ignatius's teachings for healing of memories, but they also did something more. Together with other insights of Francis concerning healing, they pointed the way to a fresh understanding of what it means to be renewed in the spirit of our mind (Eph 4:23).

In the same interview where he discussed the Spiritual Exercises, Francis spoke about why he admired the early Jesuit Peter Faber, whom he would soon declare a saint. Since you can tell a lot about a man by his friends—including his friends in heaven—I began to read Faber's spiritual diary, the *Memoriale*, to see what it might tell me about Francis's spirituality. That too was a revelation.

I found in Faber a man who had many of the same vulnerabilities as me. He battled anxiety, depression, and temptations to sin. Learning how he conquered those weaknesses helped me to better fight my own spiritual battles.

As I continued to research the wisdom of Pope Francis on healing of memories, and the Jesuit roots from which it sprang, something happened to me that was completely unexpected.

I was expecting inspiration. I was not expecting *grace*.

But grace is what I experienced. This book that you are now reading, although it began as an effort to answer my readers' desire, ended up answering my own desire for greater intimacy with Christ. Pope Francis and the Jesuits who inspired him took me on a journey that has brought me to a deeper understanding of the mercy of God—the mercy that both forgives and heals.

My hope and prayer is that, as you read this book, you too will find that healing grace—the grace that, as Francis says, enables us "to enter into dialogue with God, to be embraced by his mercy and then to bring that mercy to others."[7]

# ACKNOWLEDGMENTS

||||||||||||||||||||||||||||||||||||||||||||||||||||||||||||||||||||||||

Thanks are due first to Fr. Gregory Gresko, O.S.B., as I neglected to acknowledge him for the generous advice, encouragement, and prayers he provided as I wrote *My Peace I Give You*. For this book, I would like to thank all who have urged me to continue writing on healing of memories, especially Br. John Luth, M.I.C.; William Doino Jr.; and Fr. Angelo Mary Geiger, F.I. Finally, I am grateful to every reader who has let me know that my work has helped him or her, and to all who have prayed for me. Each of my readers is in my prayers every day, at every Mass.

# 1

# RECEIVE, O LORD, ALL MY LIBERTY

*Surrendering Your Heart to the Divine Mercy*

||||||||||||||||||||||||||||||||||||||||||||||||||||||||||||||||||||

The year was 1957 and the month was August—the dead of winter in Argentina. Jorge Mario Bergoglio, the young seminarian who would become Pope Francis, lay on a hospital bed. He was in agony, and he thought he was going to die.[1]

Jorge was in his second year at the Buenos Aires diocesan seminary, trying to discern whether to continue studying for the diocesan priesthood or to enter a religious order, when he fell ill with pneumonia. The doctors were tortuously slow to diagnose him; for three days, he was at death's door. At one point, delirious with fever, he reached up from his sickbed to embrace his mother, pleading, "Tell me, what's happening to me!"[2]

Finally, the doctors determined it was necessary to remove three pulmonary cysts and a small part of Jorge's right lung. They waited until his condition stabilized and then performed the operation.

After the procedure came more pain. For days, a saline solution was pumped into the stricken seminarian's body to clean out the affected tissue, draining out through a tube in his chest. It felt to Jorge as though salt were being poured into his wounds.

Family and friends stopped by his bedside during the ordeal, but their efforts to cheer him fell flat. Witnessing his agony, they offered trite sayings such as, "This will pass," or, "Won't it be nice when you're back home?"[3]

Perhaps Bergoglio had the trauma of that hospitalization in mind when, years later, he reflected upon our reluctance to encounter the "suffering flesh" of our neighbor: "Many do not draw near at all; they keep a distance, like the Levite and the priest in the parable [of the good Samaritan]. Others draw close by intellectualizing the pain or taking refuge in platitudes ('life's like that'). Still others focus their vision narrowly and see only what they want to see. . . . Many are the ways we avoid drawing near to flesh in pain."[4]

When, as archbishop of Buenos Aires, Bergoglio told his biographers the story of his youthful illness, he included a fond remembrance of a special visitor to his sickbed—the only one who gave him something more than platitudes. It was Sr. Dolores Tortolo, a Mercy nun who had been dear to him ever since she prepared him for First Communion. "She told me something that truly struck me and made me feel at peace: 'You are imitating Christ.'"[5]

That changed everything. It changed the way Jorge experienced the trauma of his illness. It changed the way he understood the meaning of the pain that had brought him almost to the point of death. And it seems to me that, most of all, when he realized his sufferings united him with the crucified Christ, it changed his understanding of the meaning of memory. From then on, whenever he reflected upon the events of his life, both the joys and the sufferings, he believed that his history was "infused with the loving gaze of God."[6] That is why today, as pope, he is able to say, "I have a dogmatic certainty: God is in every person's life."[7]

## A "PRAYER FULL OF MEMORY"

Soon after leaving the hospital, Jorge made the decision to enter the Society of Jesus, beginning his novitiate (the first stage of the order's formation) on March 11, 1958. He had gotten to know members of the Jesuits while attending the diocesan seminary, which they operated, and was drawn to the society's missionary spirit, community, and discipline.[8] But it was not until he became a Jesuit himself that he learned how the society's spirituality would enable him to deepen his imitation of Christ, for it was then, as a first-year novice,[9] that he made his first "Long Retreat."

The Long Retreat is the thirty-day silent retreat during which the Jesuit novice is led through the

Spiritual Exercises of St. Ignatius of Loyola.[10] Through reflecting upon the mysteries of Jesus' life, death, and resurrection, the retreatant is moved to deepen his union with God in Christ, discern his divinely appointed mission in life, and place himself fully in the divine service.[11]

Bergoglio's experience of the Spiritual Exercises—both during his Long Retreat and during the periodic retreats he would make over the ensuing years—profoundly affected his understanding of prayer. In his first major interview as pope, he told fellow Jesuit Father Antonio Spadaro, "Prayer for me is always a prayer full of memory, of recollection, even the memory of my own history. . . . For me it is the memory of which St. Ignatius speaks in the First Week of the exercises in the encounter with the merciful Christ crucified. And I ask myself: 'What have I done for Christ? What am I doing for Christ? What should I do for Christ?' It is the memory of which Ignatius speaks in the [*Contemplatio ad amorem*] when he asks us to recall the gifts we have received."[12]

The examples of Ignatian prayer that Francis cites are effectively the bookends of the Spiritual Exercises: the encounter with Christ crucified is part of the first exercise, while the *Contemplatio ad amorem*—"Contemplation to Attain the Love of God"—is the last. Together they form the spiritual framework within which the retreatant opens his mind and heart to the guidance of the Holy Spirit. Since these two meditations are so important to Francis's understanding of prayer, it is worth taking a closer look at each one.

# THE "ENCOUNTER WITH THE MERCIFUL CHRIST CRUCIFIED"

"Imagine Christ our Lord present before you on the Cross."[13]

Those words from the first meditation in the Spiritual Exercises mark the first of many times in that regimen of prayer that Ignatius invites retreatants to picture themselves face-to-face with Jesus. One could even say that the entire program of the exercises is designed to enable participants to encounter Christ directly, in the present moment. Why then does Francis, in discussing the "encounter with the merciful Christ crucified," speak of that meditation as though it were a matter of calling to mind something that is past? Why does he call it a "prayer full of memory"?

The answer, I believe, has to do with another point Francis makes in Spadaro's interview: "God is first; God is always first and makes the first move."[14]

Francis has elsewhere put the point across by using a Spanish word that turns "first" into a verb: *primerea*. To *primerea* someone is to beat him to the prize; it is a playful term normally used to describe someone who is a bit of a rascal. When Francis uses the term to speak of encountering Christ, he is making a statement akin to the observation in C. S. Lewis's Narnia books that Aslan—the character who represents God—is not a tame lion. "God awaits us to surprise us," Francis says.[15] "Letting oneself be led by Jesus leads to the surprises of Jesus."[16] In a similar way, just as Lewis wrote that his conversion left him "surprised by joy," so too Francis speaks of how God surprises us with his grace: "Grace [is] always *primerea*, grace always comes first, then comes all the rest."[17]

Behind the pope's insight is the message of 1 John 4:19: "We love because he first loved us."[18] God created us for union with him, and he sustains us in being so that we might seek and find him. Our encounter with him gives us the eyes to see how he has already been present throughout our lives. Another Francis, the poet Francis Thompson, portrayed this phenomenon in "The Hound of Heaven." Surrendering to Jesus' love after years of fleeing him, Thompson marvels, "Is my gloom, after all, / Shade of His hand, outstretched caressingly?"[19]

At the same time, it is important to note that Francis emphasizes that his "prayer full of memory" consists of more than just his own remembrance of God: "Above all, I also know that the Lord remembers me. I can forget about him, but I know that he never, ever forgets me."[20]

## MEMORY AND THE MASS

Our remembrance of God and his remembrance of us meet in the supreme "prayer full of memory," the one that unites all our individual prayers into a single offering: the holy sacrifice of the Mass.[21] Pope Paul VI employed the word "re-present" to describe how, as Christ's power operates through the actions of the priest, the past breaks through into the present. The Lord, he said, "re-presents the sacrifice of the Cross and applies its salvific power at the moment when he becomes sacramentally present—through the words of consecration—as the spiritual food of the faithful, under the appearances of bread and wine."[22]

Pope Francis has the same thought in mind when he says, "The Eucharistic Celebration is much more than simple banquet: it is exactly the memorial of Jesus' Paschal Sacrifice, the mystery at the center of salvation."[23] He emphasizes that the word "memorial," when applied to the Mass, "does not simply mean a remembrance, a mere memory": "It means that every time we celebrate this Sacrament we participate in the mystery of the passion, death, and resurrection of Christ. The Eucharist is the summit of God's saving action: the Lord Jesus, by becoming bread broken for us, pours upon us all of his mercy and his love, so as to renew our hearts, our lives and our way of relating with him and with the brethren."[24]

Over time, as we continue to bring our own, God-given capacity for memory into the memorial of Jesus' saving action, it changes us. We find that, even as we give God our memory, he is giving us his. When we have occasion to revisit images of the past that were once streaked with shadow, we are surprised to find that even the darkest patches begin to bear hints of the bright hues of the Easter sunrise. We may still feel lonely at times, but we can never again truly be alone, for we belong to Christ as members of his Mystical Body, the Church.

Francis says, "Precisely in the darkness, it is Christ that conquers and lights the fire of love."[25] Those words have particular meaning for me, for they encapsulate how I experience healing of my own memories in and through the prayers of the Mass.

Although I was not drawn to the Catholic Church until my late thirties,[26] many of my childhood memories center upon a house of worship—the Jewish temple my parents attended. It was there, before my parents split up, that we prayed as a family; it was there that my father remarried; and it was there that I witnessed my sister become recognized as a bat mitzvah when, at the age of thirteen, she read from the Torah for the first time. And it was there, when I was five years old, that I had one of my earliest experiences of evil, when the temple's janitor molested me.[27]

When I consider the fallout that the abuse caused in my young life—including the shame of being disbelieved by the rabbi after I reported what happened—I wonder how my Jewish faith was able to stand firm. Yet, it did, at least for a time, and even grew stronger.

I remember how I loved approaching the dinner table on Friday evening, the beginning of the Jewish Sabbath, to help my mother light the Shabbat candles and say the blessing that set off the holy day from the rest of the week. We would then sing the blessings over the *challah*—a special bread—and the Kiddush cup, which was filled with sweet wine.

And I remember how, after dinner, I looked forward to the Shabbat temple service. From the time I learned how to read, I was following along with the liturgy, eager to discover what was the weekly *parsha* (the reading from the Five Books of Moses) and *haftarah* (the reading from the Prophets). Only later, after my home situation degenerated and I endured new incidents of abuse, did I drift away from devotion.

So, when I think back to the temple of my childhood hometown, I remember the pain, but I also remember the beauty. The Kiddush blessing was part of the temple service as well as the home ritual, and at my temple the children were invited to come up to join the cantor in singing it. With childlike enthusiasm, I sang in Hebrew the prayer praising God's remembrance of us, a remembrance suffused with love: *"V'shabat kad'sho b'ahavah uv'ratzon hin'chilanu zikaron l'ma'aseih v'rei'sheet, . . . zeikher litzi'at Mitz'rayim."* ("You have lovingly and willingly given us your holy Shabbat as an inheritance, in memory of creation . . . [and] in memory of the exodus from Egypt.")[28]

Another recollection from the Shabbat service that stands out is reciting the *Kedushah*, which began, *"Kadosh, Kadosh, Kadosh, Adonai Tz'vaot."* The Hebrew words are from Isaiah 6:3: "Holy, Holy, Holy, Lord of Hosts."

What especially appealed to my young mind was that the *Kedushah* was more than just a vocal prayer; it engaged the whole body. Not only was it prayed standing, but also, at each *"Kadosh,"* worshipers would raise their heels to stand on the balls of their feet—lifting themselves toward heaven in union with the angels' song of praise.

Such was the angelic nature of my childhood faith— until I lost my taste for the things of heaven. As I entered

adolescence, my prayers became perfunctory. The evils I
had endured led me to doubt God's goodness. I became
attracted to the idea of living without religion and its
rules. Although the memory of my previous devotion
prevented me from denying God completely, I came to
believe that if God did exist, he did not love me. And so
it was that, from my midteens until I received the light
of Christian faith, I lived in a state of agnosticism—or,
truth be told, practical atheism.

When I first began attending Mass, I often found
myself feeling grief over things I could not change. I
would hear the priest say at the start of the Eucharistic
Prayer, "Lift up your hearts," and would feel sad about
the times in the past when I failed to lift up my heart
to God. It was as though, in the back of my mind, the
darkness of my former agnosticism remained. I would
not have dared to address God with my doubt, but if I
had, it would have come out like this: *If you really loved
me, you wouldn't have allowed me to drift so far from you
for so many years.*

But over time, as I began to enter more deeply into
the prayers of the Mass, something changed in me. Divine
grace led me to think less about my past failures and
more about the Divine Mercy. Instead of recalling the
times I doubted, I started to recall the earlier times—the
years of my childhood when I felt certain of God's love.

I don't remember exactly when it happened, but
there came a time when, praying the Sanctus—"Holy,
Holy, Holy . . ."—I realized that, during my childhood,
the Lord had given me the grace of joining in the

angels' song of prayer when I had prayed the *Kedushah*. Although I did not know as a child what I know now— that the angels exclaim their adoration as they stand before the thrice-holy Trinity (Rv 8:2)—I loved God then as I understood him, and he accepted that love.

Likewise, there came a time when, hearing the priest consecrate the Precious Blood—"Do this in memory of me"—and watching him raise the chalice, I thought back to my childhood joy at joining in the Kiddush. My heart was lifted up to the Lord then as it is now. It is true that I had less to give, because I could not return Jesus' own love back to him as I can now that he lives in me through my Baptism. Yet, I gave God all I had—my "widow's mite" (Mk 12:41–44)—and he accepted it then as he does now.

Finally, there came a time, during the Eucharistic Prayer at a daily Mass, when I looked at the altar—taking in the two candles, the bread, and the wine—and thought back to the Shabbat dinners of my childhood.

In my mind, I contrasted my memory of the Shabbat candles, which were always placed side by side, with the arrangement before me at Mass, where the candles were situated at opposite ends of the altar. As the priest— acting sacramentally in the person of Christ—stood between the candles and consecrated the bread and wine, it suddenly seemed to me that what I was seeing was a lifting of the veil.

It was as though the Shabbat candles on my family's dinner table had parted like a curtain to reveal the true liturgical action that had been happening all along in heaven while my loved ones and I had been praying here on earth. I perceived that the Mass had always been going on, but I had lacked the eyes to see it. Jesus had been there with me on Shabbat, "in the midst of the lampstands" (Rv 1:13), making his eternal offering to the Father through the Holy Spirit, and I did not know it.

I don't mean to imply that, in a true sacramental sense, my family's Jewish practice was equivalent to Catholic liturgy with chicken soup on the side. Shabbat dinner is not the Mass. Even so, Jesus is Lord of the Sabbath (Mt 12:8); it belongs to him. Through the Mass, I began to see that the joy I took in celebrating the Sabbath as a child was the beginning of my own belonging to him. My Kiddush song was a prelude to the praise I would give when I became totally his through my Baptism and reception into the Church.

The realization filled me with gratitude, for it provided a powerful answer to my unspoken doubts about God's love for me during the times when I had failed to acknowledge him. It enabled me to see my years of agnosticism not as cause to wallow in shame but rather as cause to thank God for drawing me up out of the pit (Ps 40:2).

## "THE MERCY OF GOD THAT SUSTAINS US"

Francis, in a book written prior to his papacy, observed that the right application of our memory can equip us to overcome personal challenges: "Our history is full of tensions: between past and present, between present and future, between time and eternity. Memory engages us with that tension and learns to read the present situation in the light of God's saving power, and when read this way, the present is turned into promise for the future."[29]

We find healing when we "read the present situation in the light of God's saving power" because doing so shows us that the memories we carry from our personal history do not tell the full story.[30] The wounds left by our past sufferings no longer define us. This is true regardless of whether they were caused by other people, or by outside circumstances, or by our own bad choices. Our memory is indeed part of our identity, but it is not the most important part. As Francis says, what most defines us is not that we remember but that we ourselves are remembered by God: "There is a passage in the Bible, from the prophet Isaiah, which says: Even should a mother forget her child—which is impossible—I will never forget you (Is 49:15). And this is true: God thinks about me, God remembers me. I am in God's memory."[31]

"God remembers me." That healing truth underlies Mary's great hymn of praise, the Magnificat: "He has helped Israel his servant, remembering his mercy, according to his promise to our fathers, to Abraham and to his descendants forever" (Lk 1:54–55). The Magnificat is truly a prayer full of memory, and, Francis notes, "as with Mary, our acts of thanksgiving, adoration, and praise found our memory in the mercy of God that sustains us."[32]

When our memory is thus rooted in the Lord's merciful love, it changes the way we perceive our bodily sufferings. It has to do so, because I do not only bring my soul to encounter Jesus in the Eucharist; I bring my body as well—for, as Francis has written, "our flesh is remembrance. And the memory of the Church is precisely the memory of the suffering flesh of God, the remembrance of the Lord's Passion, the Eucharistic Prayer."[33]

At the heart of the Eucharistic Prayer are Jesus' words, "This is my Body. . . . This is my Blood." When I hear Jesus say those words through the voice of the priest at Mass, if I respond in my heart by giving Jesus *my* body, *my* blood—my very heart and soul—then my own memories become joined in a special way to the memories of God.

## THE ANIMA CHRISTI: ENCOUNTERING THE FATHER THROUGH JESUS' WOUNDS

Francis's own experience of the "memory of the suffering flesh of God" is shaped by a prayer from the First Week of the Spiritual Exercises: the Anima Christi. He once observed to his fellow Jesuits that "in the Anima Christi, [Ignatius] places us in contact with the Lord's sanctifying body in such a way that we are hidden in his wounds and thus have our own wounds and sores healed."[34]

Ignatius instructs the retreatant to place himself in the presence of Jesus and make the prayer,

Soul of Christ, sanctify me.
Body of Christ, save me.
Blood of Christ, inebriate me.
Water from the side of Christ, wash me.
Passion of Christ, strengthen me.
O good Jesus, hear me.
Within Thy wounds hide me.
Suffer me not to be separated from Thee.
From the malicious enemy defend me.
In the hour of death call me,
And bid me come unto Thee,
That with Thy saints I may praise Thee
For ever and ever. Amen.

This is a prayer that bespeaks intense intimacy with Christ. The intimacy is real; it is physical; it is *enfleshed*. At the same time, the Anima Christi's imagery does not stop at Jesus' humanity; it reaches all the way to his divinity. When we ask Jesus to hide us in his wounds, we realize, as Francis has said, "That body, those wounds, those flesh—all are intercession. . . . It is through the wounds of Christ that we encounter the Father."[35]

In his first Divine Mercy Sunday homily as pope, Francis drew upon the Anima Christi's spirituality to shed light upon the passage in John's gospel where the risen Christ shows his wounds to Thomas (Jn 20:19–31). Jesus' interaction with the doubting apostle is an example of how "God responds to our weakness by his patience." "This is the reason for our confidence, our hope," Francis says, for "we too can enter into the wounds of Jesus, we can actually touch him. This happens every time that we receive the sacraments with faith." But we must have "the courage to trust in Jesus' mercy, to trust in his patience, to seek refuge always in the wounds of his love."[36]

Francis is not afraid to admit his own woundedness in order to draw fellow wounded souls to the Divine Mercy. As cardinal, he told his biographers, "I don't want to mislead anyone—the truth is that I'm a sinner who God in his mercy has chosen to love in a privileged manner."[37] Likewise, as pope, when he urges the faithful to seek refuge in Jesus' wounds, he draws upon his own personal encounters with God's saving love: "In my own life, I have so often seen God's merciful countenance, his patience; I have also seen so many people find the courage to enter the wounds of Jesus by saying to him: Lord, I am here, accept my poverty, hide my sin in your wounds, wash it away with your blood. And I have always seen that God did just this—he accepted them, consoled them, cleansed them, loved them."[38]

In describing what he has personally experienced and witnessed, Francis provides a model for our own healing: to call to mind our personal history, recognizing our need for Jesus' merciful love, and to bring our wounded lives into the arms of our wounded Savior.

What is it about Francis that enables him to be so confident that the personal history we each carry— including all the sins we have committed and all the evils we have suffered—is valuable to God? His hope is informed by another prayer from the Spiritual Exercises, part of the second meditation that he cited to Spadaro as a "prayer full of memory": the Contemplation to Attain the Love of God.

## THE SUSCIPE: WHERE MEMORY BECOMES AN OFFERING

The Contemplation to Attain the Love of God is centered upon a prayer known after its first word in Latin as the *Suscipe* (pronounced "sushi-pay"). Unlike the Anima Christi, the Suscipe was composed by St. Ignatius of Loyola himself and reflects his personal journey.[39]

When Ignatius underwent a dramatic spiritual conversion in 1521 at the age of thirty, there were many things in his past that he would have liked to forget. His mother died when he was just a baby, and soon afterward his father sent him away from the family home, to be raised by a wet nurse. Although he grew to feel at home in his nurse's family, the experiences of loss and upheaval at such a young age likely took an emotional toll on the saint.

What we know for certain is that Ignatius bore deep regrets for things he had brought upon himself. He would later say that, before he was awakened to the love of Christ, he was "a man given to worldly vanities" who became a soldier so he could satisfy "a vain and overpowering desire to gain renown."[40] We also have his friends' account that he was reckless with games, women, and brawls.

During the year following his conversion, Ignatius began an intense period of prayer and penance. It was then that he began writing his Spiritual Exercises. At the conclusion of the regime of meditations, he placed the Contemplation to Attain the Love of God.

The contemplation begins with two points for reflection: First, "love should be manifested in deeds rather than words." Second, "love consists in a mutual sharing of goods. . . . One always gives to the other."[41]

Ignatius then invites us to set the scene for the meditation: "To behold myself standing in the presence of God our Lord and of his angels and saints, who intercede for me."[42] The object will be to ask for "an intimate knowledge of the many blessings received, that filled with gratitude for everything, I may in all things love and serve the Divine Majesty."[43]

But how exactly are we to serve the Divine Majesty? What is it that God desires from us? Ignatius provides the answer through the powerful words of his Suscipe:

> Take, O Lord, and receive my entire liberty,
> my memory, my understanding, and my
>     whole will.
> All that I am and all that I possess you have
>     given me:
> I surrender it all to you to be disposed of
>     according to your will.
> Give me only your love and your grace;
> with these I will be rich enough, and will
>     desire nothing more.

Given the saint's sorrow over sinful choices he made during his former life, it is moving to see that the first thing Ignatius offers in the prayer is his liberty. Wanting to live for God instead of for himself, he gives up his freedom to act, so that he might say with St. Paul, "I have been crucified with Christ; yet I live, no longer I, but Christ lives in me" (Gal 2:19–20).

Then comes the aspect of the Suscipe that is perhaps the most striking. Having given his freedom, Ignatius seeks to give God his mind and heart. What is the first part of his inner self that he offers? It is his *memory*.

In Ignatius's understanding of the human mind, the concept of memory refers to more than just particular memories. Memory includes everything that had entered into his consciousness to make him who he was—whether or not he could actually remember it. It forms the foundation of his present identity, including his hopes for his future.

This is an ancient way of understanding memory, dating back at least to St. Augustine, and it makes particular sense for one who has survived trauma—as Ignatius had, having been wounded during his military days. Often in survivors of trauma, the brain attempts to protect itself by consigning painful swaths of the past to areas where memory's tendrils cannot reach them. Yet, the memories of traumatic events, whether present to us or not, remain part of us.

That is why there is something very beautiful about St. Ignatius offering his memory to God. The saint acknowledges there are things he cannot change—the events of his past—and at the same time displays the bold hope that his Maker will accept him as he is now, with everything he did and everything that was done to him.

## PASSING OVER FROM A "SLAVE MEMORY" TO FREEDOM IN CHRIST

I remember how arresting it was for me, as a survivor of childhood sexual abuse, when I read the words of the Suscipe for the first time. I thought, "How could God possibly want my memories? *I* don't want my memories! I have been trying to forget them. And God *wants* them?"

But the answer is that God wants everything. Most of all, as Francis says, "He wants to teach us to be more loving; he wants to confirm in us the commitment we have made, and this is what our memory does, for memory is a grace of the Lord's presence in our apostolic lives."[44] That is why Francis tells us our prayer "needs to be permeated with memory."[45] When we unite our memories to the memory of God, who remembers us, we find our identity as children of our heavenly Father in Jesus Christ, who suffered death and was buried and rose again.

And this brings us back to the first part of Ignatius's Suscipe—when he offers God his liberty. Francis observes that liberty and memory—the foundations of Ignatius's self-offering—are intimately connected. He points to a passage in the book of Deuteronomy, when Moses reminds the Israelites how the Lord, after freeing them from slavery in Egypt, provided for them during the forty years when they were being led through the

wilderness to the Promised Land: "The LORD your God
. . . fed you with manna, a food unknown to you" (Dt
8:2–3). In this way, Francis says, "the Scriptures urge the
people to recall, to remember, to memorize, the entire
walk through the desert, in times of famine and desper-
ation. The command of Moses is to return to the basics,
to the experience of total dependence on God, when
survival was placed in his hands, so the people would
understand that 'man does not live by bread alone, but
that man lives by everything that proceeds out of the
mouth of the Lord' (Dt 8:3)."[46]

If we dream of foods other than the bread of life,
Francis adds, we are "like the Hebrews in the desert,
who longed for the meat and onions they ate in Egypt,
but forgot that they had eaten those meals at the table
of slavery. In those moments of temptation, they had a
memory, but a sick memory, a selective memory. A slave
memory, not a free one."[47]

The pope's words pose a special challenge to those of
us who have suffered trauma. If we have been wounded
by others or have endured other kinds of hardship, we
may be tempted to self-pity, despair, or anger. How can
we escape such thoughts, based as they are upon evils
of the past that cannot be undone?

Francis gives us an answer with another image from
Deuteronomy. The Israelites were led from slavery to
freedom by God himself going before them, guiding
them with a pillar of cloud by day and a pillar of fire by
night (Ex 13:21). We can likewise escape our slavery to
past regrets and resentments, Francis says, if we "follow

Jesus truly present in the Eucharist." This is the true
bread from heaven—"our manna, through which the
Lord gives himself to us."[48]

Let us pray with these words of Francis: "Jesus,
defend us from the temptation of worldly food which
enslaves us, tainted food; purify our memory, so it isn't
imprisoned in selfish and worldly selectivity, but that it
may be a *living memory of your presence* throughout the
history of your people, a memory that makes a 'memorial' of your gesture of redeeming love."[49]

# 2

# TAKE MY MEMORY, MY UNDERSTANDING, AND MY ENTIRE WILL

*Entering into the Spirit of the Liturgy*

||||||||||||||||||||||||||||||||||||||||||||||||||||||||||||||||||||

On December 17, 2013, Fr. Adolfo Nicolás, superior general of the Society of Jesus, picked up his phone and heard a familiar voice—though it wasn't someone who called him every day.

"Olá, Nico, aqui Francisco . . ."

A Jesuit writer tells us what happened next, sharing a story that is now legendary among members of the Society of Jesus: "Francis added, 'I've just signed the document.' Fr. Nicolás knew immediately what document Francis was referring to—it was the one declaring Blessed Pierre Favré a saint, without all the fuss of a huge canonization ceremony."[1]

Who was Peter Faber (as Favré is known in the English-speaking world)? And why did Francis use his papal pen to canonize him without a ceremony and without even waiting for verification of a miracle taking place through his intercession?[2]

Part of the answer is that Faber, who died in 1546, has long been considered holy as well as historically significant. He was among the small circle of companions of St. Ignatius of Loyola who, with Ignatius and under his guidance, founded the Society of Jesus. But that still doesn't explain why, of all the Jesuits not yet canonized, Francis chose to elevate this one—a humble figure who is little known outside the Society of Jesus.

The fuller answer is that Francis looks to Faber as a model, admiring his personality and spirituality—including what the pope calls his "careful interior discernment."

## SPIRITUAL DISCERNMENT: LISTENING TO THE VOICE WITHIN

I remember that, as a new convert, having spent five years as a Protestant before entering the Catholic Church, I had a hard time getting a handle on what Catholics meant by "discernment." People I met who were well schooled in the faith used the word not only for mulling over concrete decisions, such as "discerning a vocation," but also for something that sounded vague and mysterious to me: "spiritual discernment."

There was, I knew, something in the Bible about testing the spirits (1 Jn 4:1). St. John discusses that concept in his first letter, advising readers on how to distinguish true prophets from false ones: "This is how you can know the Spirit of God: every spirit that acknowledges Jesus Christ come in the flesh belongs to God, and every spirit that does not acknowledge Jesus does not belong to God" (1 Jn 4:2–3).

However, what Catholics meant by spiritual discernment did not seem to concern words spoken by others. It seemed rather to concern the words spoken by one's own inner voice. This was new to me, and I was curious to learn how it differed from the teachings of psychology, some of which involve learning to identify and manage one's "self-talk."

As I did more reading on Catholicism, I learned that the Church has a long tradition of wisdom on spiritual discernment, beginning with the Bible and continuing through the writings of countless saints and mystics. But by far the most widely cited expert on the topic is a sixteenth-century saint—none other than Ignatius of Loyola, whose Spiritual Exercises includes rules for spiritual discernment.

Faber had the great privilege of learning the Spiritual Exercises from Ignatius himself. But the student outpaced his master—and this we know from Ignatius, who said that Faber was better than anyone at directing retreatants.[3]

It would be safe to say that Faber's talent for interior discernment was founded in his deep understanding of Ignatian spirituality. But he also had gifts of his own that enabled him to put the rules of the Spiritual Exercises into action in ways beyond what Ignatius conceived. An incident that Faber relates in the *Memoriale*, his spiritual diary, gives insight into why Francis finds him worthy of emulation.

It was March 1545, and Faber was staying in Valladolid, Spain, where the prince and his wife had their royal court. He arrived at the palace early one morning, intending to go to Mass at the prince's chapel, where there was a preacher he wanted to hear. But the porter, not recognizing him, refused him entrance.

Reading this story, I can easily imagine what I might have done, were I in Faber's place and denied entrance by some imperial bouncer. I might have insisted on speaking to the porter's supervisor. Failing that, I might have looked for a friend nearby—someone known to the porter—who could explain that I deserved entrance. If those tactics didn't work, I might have loitered by the door, stewing in frustration.

Faber did as I might have. Well, sort of. He loitered by the door. But to be honest, the resemblance ends there. Let us hear the rest of the story from Faber himself:

> I remained there at the door for a while, remembering that I had often allowed various sinful thoughts and evil spirits to enter my soul while leaving Jesus with his words and his Spirit to knock and stand at the door.
>
> I also reflected on how Christ had been so ill received everywhere in the world. And I prayed that it be granted the porter and me not to stand and wait for too long before the

gates of paradise, undergoing purification.
Many other thoughts, too, came to me in that
place, causing me deep remorse. So it happened that I came to love the porter all the
more, he being the cause of my devotion.[4]

This is a truly remarkable passage. It will do us good
to linger for a moment, as though we were outside the
door with Faber and he were sharing these intimate
thoughts with us personally.

The first thing the incident tells us is that Faber
lives in such deep union with God that he takes the
things that are unavoidable in life as heaven-sent teaching moments. His response to the porter's rejection is
not self-centered; it is God-centered. Instead of asking
himself how he could avoid being shut out next time,
he searches his mind for reasons why he *deserved* to be
shut out.

Note too that, as Faber seeks to discern what God
wishes to teach him through this uncomfortable incident, his mind turns to scripture. The image of "leaving
Jesus with his words and his Spirit to knock and stand
at the door" comes from the book of Revelation, where
Christ says, "Behold, I stand at the door and knock. If
anyone hears my voice and opens the door, (then) I will
enter his house and dine with him, and he with me" (Rv
3:20).

But Faber does not think only of the times he has
shut Jesus out. He also thinks of how, despite his sinfulness, God has shown him mercy and has called him
to live in imitation of Christ. So he turns his mind to

contemplate how he might experience his rejection in union with Jesus, who "had been so ill received everywhere in the world."[5]

Contemplating Christ's own experience of rejection brings Faber back to his need for Christ's mercy. But now something is in his thoughts that wasn't there previously: he seeks mercy not only for himself but also for the *porter*, whom he sees as his equal before God: "I prayed that it be granted the porter and me not to stand and wait for too long before the gates of paradise, undergoing purification." Reading those words, we can almost see Faber's heart expand before our eyes.

His heart will expand further still. As Faber is hit with "deep remorse" for his own sins, he is no longer content to even have the porter on merely equal footing with himself. Rather, he *loves* the porter, because this man, as an instrument of divine providence (however unwitting), inspired him to have feelings of devotion that he would not have otherwise enjoyed.

## A HARD-WON SERENITY

If I did not know better, I would be tempted to think that perhaps Faber was able to respond in such a holy manner because he did not face the same sort of inner challenges that I face.

During my childhood, as an early reader, I stood out as a "brainy" kid. My precociousness, as well as my being physically uncoordinated and emotionally hypersensitive, made me an easy target for certain cruel schoolmates' taunts.

Even though the teasing took place decades ago, memories of it remain embedded in my psyche. As a result, at times today when I feel excluded or snubbed, the experience is liable to trigger past pain—taking me back to when I was a vulnerable child. The idea of seeing a personal rejection as a gift from God, and even loving the person who rejects me, does not strike me as an especially easy thing to do.

So, as I said, I might imagine Faber was able to act as he did because he had fewer strikes against him—if I did not know better. His life was that of a missionary; he was constantly being moved from one place to another. An authority on his life observes that his nonstop traveling brought him "psychological suffering": "He arrived a stranger in a country, new to its customs and its ways of thinking. In Germany, for instance, he never learned German; instead, he spoke Latin or faulty Spanish, or made use of an interpreter when needed. Each new center [of operations] meant a fresh adaptation, and each new posting took him away from friends."[6]

Along with the isolation of being a foreigner, Faber also endured another kind of psychological suffering, that of recurrent depression and sadness. Much of the *Memoriale* is taken up with his efforts to find God in his mental trials. Witness this desperate prayer, inspired by the story of Jesus healing the woman who had been "crippled by a spirit" (Lk 13:10–17): "Feeling a keen spiritual desire and with a heightened consciousness of what I might call the cringing and despondent state of my spirit, I begged for an elevation of my mind through grace so that, instead of being habitually stooped and drawn downward in its abjection toward that 'spirit which causes its infirmity,' it might through the grace of Christ devote itself rather to growing in that life which consists in 'looking ever upwards.'"[7]

When I read passages like that, I realize how wrong it would be to assume that the saint was blissfully free from interior conflict. Clearly, Faber's serenity was hard won, the fruit of ongoing prayer, discernment, and self-discipline. But how, exactly, did he fight his spiritual battle?

A careful reading of the *Memoriale* reveals that Faber's healing took place as he applied the spirituality of Ignatius's exercises in a manner distinctly his own.

## SETTING YOUR HEART TO THE LITURGICAL RHYTHMS

As we saw in chapter 1, the exercises bring the retreatant into an encounter with Christ through bringing him or her to contemplate the mysteries of Christ's life. Faber brought that same level of contemplation into his daily life, and he did it through attuning himself to the liturgical rhythms of the Church—that is, to Sunday Mass, and to the times and seasons that have been appointed for the various feasts. Whatever the Church was celebrating on a given day—be it a saint's feast, a holy day, or just a daily Mass in what we would now call "ordinary time"—he entered into that celebration spiritually. As he entered into it, he desired with all his heart to unite his thoughts and feelings to the person or event being commemorated.

I use the phrase "liturgical rhythms" intentionally. It captures how Faber put his entire person into the Church's celebrations—and I don't mean this simply because he, in the priestly act, made Jesus Christ present in the Eucharist. I mean that the celebrations of the Church—from Sunday to Sunday, from Easter to Easter, and from Christmas to Christmas—held command over Faber's spiritual rhythms in the way that daytime and nighttime command the human person's biological rhythms.

We could even say that, in a spiritual sense, Faber's heart beat to those liturgical rhythms. In his *Memoriale*, when he describes his interior movements on Fridays and other days commemorating Jesus' passion, he is always straining to place himself within the Passion, and to place the Passion within himself. His spirituality was that of the Anima Christi, so beloved by Ignatius, with its plea, "Within thy wounds, hide me." Likewise, on Sundays and joyful feasts, Faber sought a more intimate understanding of the Resurrection, so that he might live in the risen Christ, and so that the risen Christ might live in him.

A section of the *Memoriale* written on Good Friday, 1543, offers a beautiful example of how Faber's method of placing himself within the Church's liturgical rhythms led him to find spiritual healing. The saint begins by relating the mental sufferings he had endured over the preceding weeks: "During the whole of Lent, I had been disturbed in various ways by thoughts and interior motions, a sign that the wounds of my miseries and imperfections were beginning to reopen."[8]

But then comes Palm Sunday, the beginning of Holy Week. As Faber examines the state of his soul on that day, he realizes that the sufferings he has borne during the Lenten season are not meaningless. Just as Jesus suffered his passion and death so that Faber and all humanity might be freed from sin, so too God enables Faber's own sufferings, offered in union with those of Christ, to work toward his purification: "[Palm Sunday] and that season consecrated to the Passion of our Lord is the time for remembering the wounds of Christ's body, his torments, his death, the insults and ignominies and mockery he suffered. It must then have been good for me that my spiritual wounds and the scars left by my infirmities (not fully healed at the time) opened, as it were, into fresh wounds from then on during that season in which we celebrate once again the sufferings and the merits of Christ."[9]

Even as he displays faith that, by God's grace, his mental suffering can serve a positive purpose, Faber refuses to romanticize his pain; he wants no more of it. So he asks God for healing. As he does so, he recognizes that his very desire to pray for that intention is a divine inspiration: "God then granted me the favor of seeking with my whole heart, through the crucifixion and death of Jesus Christ, a remedy for those many great infirmities of mine."[10]

When Good Friday comes around, Faber's prayer becomes bolder. He wants the day of Christ's resurrection also to be that of his own spiritual resurrection: "I resolved to offer the Mass I intended to celebrate on the coming Saturday [Easter Vigil] to obtain from God the grace of a rebuilding and refashioning of myself in some worthy way."[11]

The last words the saint writes before going to bed that Good Friday night show that, even as he contemplates Jesus on the Cross, his heart is expanding with the hope of Easter: "While I was contemplating the body of Christ in the tomb, lifeless yet united to the divinity, a great desire led me to ask that all the power of sin in me . . . might be brought to nothing, and I asked as well the grace of possessing life in God through Jesus Christ our Lord, risen from the dead."[12]

## THE TRANSFIGURATION OF TIME

Although Faber's approach to prayer is distinctive, informed by Ignatian spirituality and by his own imagination, the idea of entering into the rhythms of the liturgy is by no means unique to him. He is simply an outstanding example of how every Christian is called to unite his spirit with the spirit of the Church's celebrations. Just as Christ's resurrection is the first fruits of the general resurrection, so too God's sanctification of time through the liturgy is the first fruits of the "perfect day" of heaven (Prv 4:18, Rv 22:5).

The *Catechism of the Catholic Church* uses the strongest possible terms to describe the liturgy's sanctification of time, going so far as to call it a *transfiguration*. "Beginning with the Easter Triduum as its source of light, the new age of the Resurrection fills the whole liturgical year with its brilliance. Gradually, on either side of this source, the year is transfigured by the liturgy" (CCC 1168).

Pope Francis's earliest experience of faith was an experience of this very transfiguration, within the radiant light of the Easter Triduum. It is a story he has told many times, involving his beloved grandmother Rosa, whom he has called "the woman who had the greatest influence on my life":[13]

> I had the great blessing of growing up in a family in which faith was lived in a simple, practical way. However it was my paternal grandmother in particular who influenced my journey of faith.
>
> She was a woman who explained to us [grandchildren], who talked to us about Jesus, who taught us the catechism. I always remember that on the evening of Good Friday she would take us to the candlelight procession, and at the end of this procession "the dead Christ" would arrive and our grandmother would make us—the children—kneel down and she would say to us: "Look, he is dead, but tomorrow he will rise." . . .
>
> This is really beautiful! And this is how I received my first experience of faith.[14]

Rosa influenced Francis's journey of faith not only by her words but also by her witness. Francis found in her a kind of holiness that he would later describe in terms of patience—"not only patience as . . . taking charge of the events and circumstances of life, but also as a constancy in going forward, day by day."[15]

In his Apostolic Exhortation *Evangelii gaudium*, Francis writes of this same virtue of patience—only there, Peter Faber is his model. To illustrate his point that those who wish to share the faith must be patient while grace does its invisible work, he quotes one of Faber's maxims: "Time is God's messenger."[16]

Faber learned the truth of that maxim in his own life as he experienced healing through the gentle action of the Holy Spirit working in his soul over time. One important moment in this process took place over December 25–27, 1542.

## ATTAINING THE LOVE THAT GOES BEYOND FEELINGS

In the *Memoriale* entry for December 25, as Faber writes about celebrating midnight Mass, we see that he began Christmas Day in a state of sadness. He had hoped to receive Jesus in the Eucharist with feelings of Christmas joy. Instead, he writes, "I was feeling cold before Communion and was grieved that my dwelling was not better prepared."[17]

Just as he was thinking those thoughts, a feeling of consolation came to him with such suddenness that he knew it could only be a gift from above. "I received this answer accompanied by an interior feeling of devotion that moved me to tears: This is what the coming of Christ into a stable means. If you were already very fervent, you would not see here the humanity of your Lord because spiritually you would correspond less to what is called a stable."[18]

As I read those words, my heart tells me the saint was right to understand them as a message from the Holy Spirit.

Note especially how the consolation points the saint toward a love that goes beyond feelings. It would have reminded Faber of Ignatius of Loyola's admonition in the Contemplation to Attain the Love of God: "Love ought to manifest itself in deeds rather than in words."[19] What matters most in love is not what we feel—because feelings can change—but what we *will*.

In his longing for feelings, Faber had focused upon his own experience of love, rather than upon the object of his love—Jesus Christ. The words of the consolation remind him that, if his heart is truly to be a stable, it has to be empty of self.

The evening after Christmas, on the vigil of the feast of St. John the Evangelist, we see Faber take the consolation's message into prayerful reflection. He thinks about how John's gospel presents John as "the one whom Jesus loved" (Jn 13:23), while Peter is the disciple who professes the greatest love for Jesus (Jn 21:15–17). Until this point, he has wanted to be like John more than he has wanted to be like the saint for whom he was named.

Now he realizes it is time to reverse his priorities: "For the future, I must take more care to do what is better and more generous and what I have done less of: to will to love rather than to will to be loved. . . . Take care to be Peter first so as then to become John, who was loved more and in greater favor."[20]

Faber's words reveal the new level of maturity he is attaining under the guidance of the Holy Spirit. In light of the consolation he received at midnight Mass, he realizes that God wants to live in a constant exchange of love with him—an exchange that can take place only if he continually seeks to expand his heart.

The dynamics of this exchange of love become clearer to the saint the following day, as the feast of St. John arrives. He reflects on how the believer first seeks to be loved by God but then, under the guidance of the Holy Spirit, is inspired "to seek and to tend not so much to be loved by God but to love him": "The first attitude of mind, then, is to draw God to us; the second, however, is to draw ourselves to God."[21]

As the saint thinks about these two attitudes, he makes a fascinating connection: they both have to do with *memory.* "In the first we seek to have [God] remember us and assume complete care of us; in the second we seek to remember him and to be fully engaged only in what pleases him."[22]

With those words, the exchange of love that Faber has described is placed within the context of time—the days of our lives. God loves us by remembering us, and he demonstrates this loving remembrance through his providential care for us, as he brings the mercies that the Psalmist says are "new every morning" (Lam 3:23, RSV). We love God in return by remembering him, and we demonstrate our remembrance of him by offering ourselves to do his will.

Where does this exchange of loving remembrance take place? Faber tells us it transpires when we practice recollection, a form of intimate personal prayer in which we find God's presence dwelling within our heart. But he is keen to add that this recollection is not possible on our own power. To attain it, we need to center our prayer life on a concrete, even physical moment of encounter with God. We find that moment in our reception of Jesus in the Eucharist—Jesus, who entered into history in order to enter into our innermost being.

"It is properly in the most holy Sacrament that the grace to attain recollection is found," Faber says. "Our Lord wishes to enter into us and lead us to conversion of heart so that by following him we may daily enter more and more into the deepest depths of ourselves."[23]

Those words of Faber bring out one of the most wondrous truths of the Christian life. God, who is outside of time, enters into our bodies and souls through Jesus in the Eucharist so that he might be with us daily, in all the times and seasons of our lives. Pope Francis tells us that "through the Eucharist, . . . Christ wishes to enter into our life and permeate it with his grace," to give us "coherence between liturgy and life."[24]

Let us ask for that grace as we make a self-examination suggested by Francis: "How do I live the Eucharist?

. . . In adoring Christ who is really present in the Eucharist: Do I let myself be transformed by him? Do I let the Lord who gives himself to me, guide me to going out ever more from my little enclosure, in order to give, to share, to love him and others?"[25]

# 3

# WHATSOEVER I HAVE OR HOLD, YOU HAVE GIVEN ME

*Sharing in Mary's Grace of Memory*

||||||||||||||||||||||||||||||||||||||||||||||||||||||||||||||||||||||||||||

One day in late 1958, as Jesuit novice Jorge Bergoglio entered into the fourth week of his first-ever experience of the thirty-day Spiritual Exercises, the future pontiff was instructed to contemplate a scene not found in any of the gospels: the risen Jesus appearing to Mary.

The contemplation appears at the beginning of a section of meditations upon Jesus' resurrection appearances. All the other ones that Ignatius lists are mentioned in the gospels: Jesus appears to Mary Magdalene (Jn 20:14), St. Peter (Lk 24:34), the disciples on the road to Emmaus (Lk 24:13), and so on. But the Jesuit founder, following a long-standing Catholic tradition, holds that before Jesus appeared to anyone else, he appeared to his Mother, to

41

console and strengthen her after the sorrow she endured witnessing the events of his passion.

Knowing that Bergoglio meditated upon Mary's encounter with her risen Son, we might wonder what kind of impact that contemplation had upon the faith of the man who would be pope. Francis himself has given us the answer, in a speech where he instructs his listeners to contemplate that very scene.

First, Francis, like Ignatius in the exercises, invites us to contemplate Mary at the foot of the Cross, where "she is at once the woman of sorrow and of watchful expectation of a mystery far greater than sorrow which is about to be fulfilled."[1] At a time when it appeared that all hope was gone, "she too, at that moment, remembering the promises of the annunciation could have said: they did not come true, I was deceived. But she did not say this. And so she who was blessed because she believed, sees blossom from her faith a new future and awaits God's tomorrow with expectation."[2]

Reflecting on Mary's patience leads Francis to consider our own need for patience: "Do we know how to wait for God's tomorrow? Or do we want it today?" Mary is our model, because "for her the tomorrow of God is the dawn of Easter morning, the dawn of the first day of the week."

This "tomorrow of God," the fulfillment of our Easter hope, is what comes to mind for Francis when he contemplates the risen Jesus' appearance to Mary. And so he invites all of us to imagine that encounter and incorporate its fruit into our lives. "It would do us good to think, in contemplation, of the embrace of Mother and Son. The single lamp lit at the tomb of Jesus is the hope of the mother, which in that moment is the hope of all humanity."

What was it about Mary that enabled her to keep the flame alive until her Son rose? We can find a clue in another title that Francis gives her: "Our Lady of Memory."[3]

## MARY REMEMBERS GOD—AND GOD REMEMBERS HER

Francis calls Mary "Our Lady of Memory" because she is the one who "from the beginning meditated on all those things in her heart"—the things the angel Gabriel told her about who she was, who Jesus was, and what Jesus would accomplish (Lk 1:26–37).[4]

In Luke's gospel, after the annunciation, we see Mary go in haste to visit her cousin Elizabeth, who had conceived a son in her old age. Elizabeth, hearing her greeting, is filled with the Holy Spirit. The child in her womb—John the Baptist—leaps for joy, and she cries out in awe (Lk 1:41–45). The final words that Luke records Elizabeth speaking to Mary are, "Blessed is she who believed that there would be a fulfillment of what was spoken to her by the Lord" (Lk 1:45, RSV).

If we pause for a moment to reflect upon that joyous proclamation, we see that Elizabeth is praising Mary for her faith, her hope, and, in a special way, her *memory*.

Mary chooses to remember the Lord's words, put her faith in them, and act upon them.

In this way, Elizabeth's words provide the context for Mary's outburst of joy, the Magnificat (Lk 1:46–55). Francis observes that "the first thing [Mary] does upon meeting Elizabeth is to recall God's work, God's fidelity, in her own life, in the history of her people, in our history: 'My soul magnifies the Lord . . . for he has looked on the lowliness of his servant. . . . His mercy is from generation to generation' (Lk 1:46, 48, 50). Mary remembers God."[5]

Note that Mary's Magnificat is not just a remembrance of what God did for others. "This canticle of Mary," Francis says, "also contains the remembrance of her personal history, God's history with her, her own experience of faith."[6]

What is true for Mary's faith is true for ours as well. "Faith contains our own memory of God's history with us, the memory of our encountering God who always takes the first step, who creates, saves and transforms us."[7]

As time went on, Mary's memory of God's history with her would include premonitions of pain. St. Luke indicates she reflected deeply upon all the events of Jesus' young life (Lk 2:19, 2:51)—including the words of Simeon, who prophesied that her soul would be pierced by sorrow for her Son's sake: "Behold, this child is set for the fall and rising of many in Israel, and for a sign that is spoken against (and a sword will pierce through your own soul also), that thoughts out of many hearts may be revealed" (Lk 2:34–35, RSV).

Pope Francis, commenting on those passages of Luke's gospel, observes that Mary permitted God to restructure her memory so that, when the day came that the sword of sorrow would pierce her heart, she would be able to stand firm. "She bore in her heart, throughout the pilgrimage of her life, the words of the elderly Simeon who foretold that a sword would pierce her soul, and with persevering strength she stood at the foot of the cross of Jesus."[8]

Mary would also hold in memory the words Jesus spoke to her in the Temple when he was twelve years old. When she asked him why he had gone missing for three days, leaving her and Joseph to search anxiously for him, he answered, "Why were you looking for me? Did you not know that I must be in my Father's house?" (Lk 2:49). We are told that even though Mary and Joseph "did not understand" these words that Jesus spoke to them, Mary again "kept all these things in her heart" (Lk 2:50, 51).

Fr. Angelo Mary Geiger, F.I., points out that Jesus' words give Mary an interpretational key: "Three days, the Father's house." After that, "she won't be surprised again. The next time Jesus is gone for three days"—as his body lies in the tomb—"she will know exactly where to find him."[9]

Keeping Jesus' words in her heart empowers Mary to move forward even when she cannot yet see how the present trauma would be resolved. Her fortitude at the foot of the Cross comes not from forgetting her past suffering but from remembering it in a new way.

# HEALING OF MEMORY: WHAT DOES THE BIBLE SAY?

Shortly after I began writing this book, in April 2015, I traveled to South Dakota to speak on healing of memories at a small Catholic parish on a Native American reservation. Much healing was needed there; the reservation was known for its high rates of child abuse, drug abuse, and suicide.

I had just finished giving my talk when a middle-aged woman in the front row raised her hand to ask a question. She was clearly hurting. Her brow was furrowed and her speech was halting. As she tried to get her words out, I admired her courage in publicly revealing her pain.

"Is there . . . anything in the Bible . . . ," she began.

*Good,* I thought. *A Bible question. I know my Bible, so I should be on safe ground.*

". . . anything in the Bible about people who recover their memory? About people who block out their memories of trauma, and then get their memories back?"

*Whoa!* I had to pause and reflect. No one had ever asked me a question like that.

A year earlier, before I began researching the thought of Pope Francis, the question would have left me stumped. There is no doubt that the Bible relates many traumatic experiences—from Adam and Eve's expulsion from Eden, all the way up to Jesus' passion and the sufferings of the early Christians. But how could it have anything to say to us about remembering forgotten pain? Wasn't that a modern phenomenon, something

that became known only after posttraumatic stress disorder (PTSD)entered the public vocabulary in the 1980s?

No, it wasn't. It was, I realized, in fact a very old
phenomenon. The woman's question touched upon an
important theme of the New Testament—one that held
particular significance for Francis.

"There are," I began, "*many* incidents in the Bible
where a person blocks out a traumatic memory and only
recalls it later. We see it all through the gospels.

"Think of all the times when Jesus, as he heads
toward Jerusalem, tells his disciples that the Son of Man
must suffer, and be rejected, and scourged, and spit upon,
and killed, and rise again on the third day.[10]

"It was *traumatic* for the disciples to hear that. First
of all, they didn't have a concept of a suffering Messiah.
They were expecting a warrior Messiah, one who would
take back Israel from the Roman occupation.[11] So the
idea of a suffering Messiah scandalized them.[12]

"What's more, the disciples loved Jesus more than
they loved anyone. Hearing him predict his own death
was as though they were hearing their own father tell
them he would be beaten, humiliated, and killed. It was
too much for them to handle.

"So what did they do? They blocked it out. And so,
when Jesus' predictions of his passion came true, the disciples were blindsided. Having never expected that their
leader would be taken away from them, they scattered.

"And with that, we see the real problem that happens
when people block out memories of past trauma. Prac-
tically every time Jesus predicted his passion, he would

also say that, after three days, he would rise. But because the disciples blocked out their memories of Jesus' predictions of his passion, they also blocked out his predictions of his *resurrection*. So, when he was crucified, their hope was gone.

"But what happens after Jesus rises? Pope Francis points out in one of his homilies that when Mary Magdalene and the other Mary came to the tomb expecting to find Jesus, and instead found it empty, the angel said to them, 'Remember what he told you when he was with you in Galilee. . . .'[13] And they remembered his words. The first thing Jesus does when he rises from the dead is that he *restores our memory*.

"Jesus' encounter with the disciples on the road to Emmaus demonstrates this beautifully.[14] The two disciples don't recognize him as he approaches them. They are speaking to one another about what just happened in Jerusalem—Jesus' crucifixion. When Jesus asks what they are discussing, their faces become downcast; they look at the ground. Isn't that like what we do when we are traumatized? We don't want other people to see our expression.

"The disciples tell Jesus about the events of the Passion, but they speak as though they had no hope. They even say that some women went to the tomb and reported that Jesus was alive, but they themselves have no memory of Jesus saying he would rise. They blocked out his predictions of his death because they couldn't imagine a suffering Messiah. You see this in their saying,

'But we were hoping that he would be the one to redeem Israel.'

"Jesus could respond by immediately revealing his identity to the disciples, but he doesn't. Instead, before showing them who he really is, he first heals their memories. He uses the words of the prophets to remind them of what he himself had said to them during his earthly life—that the Messiah would enter into his glory through suffering."

Having said all this, I thanked the woman for her question, and she seemed to take comfort in my response. Only afterward did I realize that, however much my words might have helped her, she had helped me more, for she inspired me to go back and reread Pope Francis's homily about the empty tomb. What I found there about how the risen Christ healed his followers' memories led me to contemplate more deeply how he heals my own memories.

## AT THE EMPTY TOMB: THE REMEMBRANCE THAT OVERCOMES FEAR

The homily I had in mind was one in which the pope speaks of the encounter that Mary Magdalene and the other women from Galilee had with the angels on the morning of the Resurrection. Finding the angels in the tomb, and no sign of Jesus' body, the women are terrified. It is then that the angels tell them what Francis notes is "something of crucial importance": "Remember what he said to you while he was still in Galilee, that the Son of Man must be handed over to sinners and be crucified, and rise on the third day. And they remembered his words" (Lk 24:6–8).

> They are asked to remember their encounter with Jesus, to remember his words, his actions, his life; and it is precisely this loving remembrance of their experience with the Master that enables the women to master their fear and to bring the message of the Resurrection to the Apostles and all the others.[15]

It is worth taking a moment to delve into the implications of Francis's insights. He suggests that, before the women at the tomb can fully appreciate and share the good news of the Resurrection, they first need to see their own personal past within the light of the Easter sunrise. They do this by remembering "their encounter with Jesus"—"his words, his actions, his life."

The women's personal memories of Jesus included traumatic events. They had heard Jesus predict his passion, and they were there when his prediction was fulfilled. But in their distress over his sufferings and death, they had forgotten his promise that, after three days, he would rise. The angels' reminder leads them to lift the mental block they had placed upon their painful past so that they could see how Jesus had always loved them, always wanted them to hope in him—and now, having risen, he would always be with them.[16]

Those thoughts bring me to contemplate anew Jesus' meeting with the disciples on the road to Emmaus.

When the disciples, thinking he was a stranger, told him about the things they had witnessed in Jerusalem, why did he not reveal his identity to them then and there? Why did he wait to show them who he was until he had first explained the meaning of past events? There is, I believe, a message here.

I think about when I first entered the Catholic Church, at a time when I was just beginning to come to terms with the abuse I had suffered during my childhood. Like the disciples on the road to Emmaus, I had encountered Jesus through faith, but my memory was streaked with shadows where the light of Christ had failed to penetrate.

As I began to live within the rhythms of the sacraments—attending Mass not just weekly but even daily and going to confession regularly—I started to sense a change in the way I perceived my personal history.

It was unnerving at first—painful memories would insinuate themselves upon my consciousness when I least expected them, sometimes even at Mass. But over time, with the help of a good spiritual director, I learned that, when unwanted memories came up, I could offer them to Jesus in the Eucharist. Just as Jesus gave me himself through the sacrament, so too, when I received him, I gave him myself—including my memories.

To put it in St. Ignatius of Loyola's terms, my past traumas became part of my Suscipe (see chapter 1). In this way too, I was like the disciples on the road to Emmaus, who entrusted Jesus with their stories of the painful events they had witnessed.

My self-offering of memory put me into a beautiful dialogue with the eucharistic Christ. As I gave Jesus my memories, I found that he was giving me his. He who, on the road to Emmaus, had restructured his disciples' memories was restructuring mine. With the aid of grace, I came to understand my sufferings in light of the sufferings of "the Son of God, who loved me and gave himself for me" (Gal 2:20, RSV).

Later on, I would find in Pope Francis's encyclical *Lumen fidei* a description of what I experienced. Francis writes that "the sacraments communicate an incarnate memory, linked to the times and places of our lives, linked to all our senses."[17]

The new understanding I received of my sufferings did not in itself heal me of the invisible wounds left by my childhood trauma. I still endured effects of trauma, including occasional anxiety, sadness, and flashbacks, which were beyond my conscious control. Taken together, my constellation of symptoms added up to PTSD. The pain of my past had long ago become embodied, and bodily symptoms cannot be simply wished away.

Yet, even as my symptoms lingered, over time I noticed there was a real difference in the manner in which I experienced the effects of past pain. When something happened that triggered unwanted memories, leading me to cry, my tears no longer had the last word. PTSD might still cause me discomfort, but it could no longer harm me. It could rankle me—because I was human, after all—but it couldn't alter my identity as a beloved child of God in Christ.

The past was not my enemy any more. I could no longer be a prisoner of fear, anger, or shame.

## THE EUCHARIST AND PURIFICATION OF MEMORY

What caused this change? It took place as I came to understand that the feelings of isolation that my painful memories evoked were just that—feelings. They were not the truth. The truth was that every time I felt the pain of any kind of wound, Jesus Christ was with me in a profound way. He was with me already, through the graces I had received in Baptism, but he was with me on an even deeper and more intimate level if I consciously asked him to be with me when I suffer.

The Church calls this a mystery. It's a mystery because, even though we know it is true, we will never get to the bottom of it. And this mysterious truth is that when I unite my own wounded heart with the wounded and glorified heart of Jesus, his wounds heal mine.

And so it was that Jesus, in healing my memory, opened my eyes so that I could better share in his resurrected life. As when, after he healed the disciples' memories on the road to Emmaus, they recognized him in the breaking of the bread, so too, the more I allow Jesus to restructure my understanding, the more I come to recognize him when I meet him in the Eucharist. It is the grace of memory that enables this recognition—a memory purified in the fire of Christ's love.

Mary had this grace of memory throughout her life. St. John Paul II observed that "in her daily preparation for Calvary, Mary experienced a kind of 'anticipated Eucharist'—one might say a 'spiritual communion'—of desire and of sacrificial offering, which would culminate in her union with her Son in his Passion."[18] She remembered her encounter with God and clung to it, so that God would always be present to her in the most intimate way—in times of pain as well as joy.

It was because of this unbroken intimacy that Mary was able to sustain the disciples' hope after Jesus' ascension, as they awaited the gift of the Holy Spirit on Pentecost, as Francis observes: "Just as her pain was intimate enough to pierce her soul, so too her joy was also intimate and deep, and the disciples were able to draw from it. Having passed through the experience of the death and Resurrection of her Son, seen in faith as the supreme expression of God's love, Mary's heart became a font of peace, consolation, hope and mercy."[19]

The Holy Father's words remind us that Mary did not have a selective memory. She chose to remember her entire encounter with Jesus, including the pain, keeping everything in her heart. But the pain did not overpower her, because, all through it, she kept the gaze of her heart fixed on Jesus. Instead of letting herself be defined by the three hours when the sun went black, she is defined by the Easter morning when the light of her risen Son, who is the "Light from Light," dawned upon the world, never to depart. She knows, as Jesus told the disciples on the road to Emmaus, that it was indeed "necessary that the Messiah should suffer these things and enter into his glory" (Lk 24:26).

The Resurrection, then, does not wipe out Mary's memory of the Passion. Rather, it *completes* her experience, equipping her to properly integrate the trauma into her identity. Her past pain becomes an integral part of her present joy. That is why "she knows the way" to healing in Christ, Francis notes, "and for this reason she is the Mother of all of the sick and suffering. To her we can turn with confidence and filial devotion, certain that she will help us, support us and not abandon us. She is the Mother of the crucified and risen Christ: she stands beside our crosses and she accompanies us on the journey towards the resurrection and the fullness of life."[20]

That is why Francis says our own memory, like Mary's, "should overflow with the wondrous things done by God."[21] "To remember what God has done and continues to do for me, for us, to remember the road we have travelled; this is what opens our hearts to hope for the future."[22]

Let us pray with Francis, asking Mary's help in obtaining this grace of memory:

> Mother, help our faith! . . .
> Sow in our faith the joy of the Risen One.
> Remind us that those who believe are never alone.
> Teach us to see all things with the eyes of Jesus, that he may be light for our path. And may this light of faith always increase in us,

until the dawn of that undying day which is
Christ himself, your Son, our Lord![23]

# 4

# I GIVE IT ALL BACK TO YOU

## *Living the Beatitudes*

In *The Thrill of the Chaste* (Catholic edition), I tell of a conversation I had with an unmarried female friend who was feeling lonely. She brought up an utterance that St. Bernadette reported during the apparitions at Lourdes, when Mary said she could promise Bernadette happiness not in this world but only in the next. The meaning my friend took from Mary's message was that she herself was not meant to have happiness in this world.

At the time, I responded as a friend would, telling her I knew God had a plan for her, a plan for her well-being and not for evil, to give her a future and hope. Afterward I realized I could have challenged her interpretation of the apparition. Mary is, after all, Our Lady of Hope. Granted, in apparitions that have been approved by the Church, including Lourdes, she urges the faithful to penance. But she always points to healing in Christ—healing that brings joy in this life. Lourdes didn't receive its reputation as one of the world's top pilgrimage sites by sending people home depressed.

What, then, did Mary mean in speaking to Bernadette? By promising happiness only in heaven, was she condemning the French teenager to a life of meaninglessness?

That is not what Bernadette thought. To gain an idea of how she understood Mary's words, we can look at a letter written in 1863, fifteen years after the Lourdes apparitions, when she was a religious sister. The author of the letter was Fr. C. Alix, a priest who had given her spiritual direction. His words meant so much to Bernadette that, ten years after receiving the letter, she transcribed it in her own hand so as to have a fresh copy of the words she had read and reread so many times.

In the letter, Fr. Alix offered Bernadette "a few thoughts on holiness" that he hoped would provide food for her meditations. Among the advice he gives, one point reads as though he were interpreting Mary's promise to her of happiness in heaven: "Give the appearance of living on earth as long as it pleases God to leave you here, but in reality, live in Heaven in your thoughts, your emotions, and your desires."[1]

How do we begin to live the life of heaven while on earth? The wisdom of the Church, throughout the ages, has answered that question by pointing to the Beatitudes. When the *Catechism* speaks of the Beatitudes, it uses words such as "already" and "even now." The language is qualified, to be sure, but it is there. We are told that the Beatitudes "proclaim the blessings and rewards already secured, however dimly, for Christ's disciples" (CCC 1717). And we are told that, even though the pure in heart will not enjoy the vision of God until the next life, "even now [purity of heart] enables us to see *according* to God, to accept others as 'neighbors'; it lets us perceive the human body—ours and our neighbor's—as a temple of the Holy Spirit, a manifestation of divine beauty" (CCC 2519).

## THE SUNRISE THAT DISPELS THE DARKNESS

Before I received faith in Jesus, I did not know these things. I knew that I wanted love, but I did not believe I was truly lovable. The abuse I suffered in childhood led me to believe I was valuable not for who I was but only for what I did. In my loneliness, I sought love in things that were not love.

Fr. Daniel A. Lord, S.J., wrote that "the whole Christian viewpoint should be colored by the sunrise of Easter."[2] In the years since I became a Christian, and especially since I entered into the fullness of faith in the Catholic Church, I have begun to see how that Easter sunrise was on the horizon even during those years when I was living as though God did not exist. There were certain moments that seem in retrospect to have been the beginning of a divine in-breaking.

One such moment stands out. It happened one night in October 1995. I was twenty-seven and suffering from what I now know was PTSD, which, as I shared earlier, was caused by the abuse I suffered in childhood. At the time, I only knew that, even though my psychiatrist had me taking three different mood medications, I was plagued by thoughts of suicide. To keep myself going, I would fix my thoughts upon some exciting event in the near future—usually a rock concert—and tell myself that I could not think of self-harm until the event had passed.

On this night in 1995, I was at one such event—a performance at a Manhattan nightclub by a touring male singer. I had admired the singer from afar for ten years, building up a romantic fantasy around him as people do with their idols.

After the concert, since I was attending in my capacity as a music journalist, I was permitted to remain at the club after the show as the singer unwound with his friends. There was a brief opportunity for me to greet the singer; he was professional and gracious. I felt a twinge of disappointment that he didn't fall in love with me there and then—though I hadn't really expected him to do so.

The only thing left for me to do was walk out onto the midnight streets and catch the underground train home. But I didn't want to go. Having used the concert as an excuse to avoid thinking of suicide, it felt as if my dark thoughts were waiting for me back home. So I lingered in the dimly lit club, feeling out of place as the singer's friends chatted with one another. Meanwhile, the singer, relieved of the pressure of putting on a show, sat on the edge of the stage with his acoustic guitar, playing and singing softly. I thought of calling out a request—there was a song of his that I was longing to hear him play—but I feared spoiling the mood.

As the singer finished playing a song, his friends stopped chatting long enough to applaud. I did too—and shyly called out my request.

At first the singer seemed not to have heard me. He retuned his guitar, while his friends resumed their conversation. Again I thought of leaving, having worn out my welcome, and again my stomach cringed in dread of going home with nothing to look forward to.

Then the singer sang his song—*my* song.

It was a kind of love song, but it was more about what it feels like to realize that you will never get to the bottom of the mystery of another person. It expressed how the beloved is present within the lover, and yet the lover can never fully contain the beloved. When I reflect on it today, the passage from Ecclesiastes comes to mind: "All rivers flow to the sea, yet never does the sea become full" (Eccl 1:7).

I remember watching the singer, listening to him, and longing to freeze that moment in time. An overpowering sense of wonder washed over me. With surprise, I was struck by the thought that the singer, in playing my request, had given me something far more intimate than if he had spent the night with me. Yet, the intimacy I felt was somehow not with him but rather with something beyond him, something that was beautiful and just out of reach.

If you had told me at that moment that I was really longing for God, I would not have believed you. I was certain that I was longing for a person, and God to me was not a person. Yet, in the depth of my soul, I felt the desire for something that could not be fulfilled by the lifestyle I was living. And at the same time, whereas normally my feelings of unfulfilled desire brought loneliness and even despair, the desire I experienced at that moment contained within itself a taste of the very thing I longed for. That, I now realize, is why I felt wonder. The desire gave me a vision of what my life would be like if I allowed God to reorder my desires. So strange and yet so familiar, it was a foretaste of the beatitude of the pure in heart.

## PUTTING YOUR OWN FACE ON THE BEATITUDES

Pope Francis uses an evocative image to describe the Beatitudes. He calls them "the Christian's identity card."[3]

The choice of metaphor is intriguing. The pope does not simply say the Beatitudes are words to live by, like a creed or a code of honor. Instead, he invites us to picture a card that features a photograph of our own face.

But there is a significant difference, I believe, between what we usually think of when we imagine an identity card and what Francis wants us to picture. Identity-card photos are often taken quickly, in bad lighting, on a day when we have been waiting in line and find it difficult to manage a sincere smile. (I speak from personal experience. My own ID photo looks like a police mug-shot.) Yet, when Francis calls the Beatitudes "the Christian's identity card," he does not want me to picture myself at my worst. Rather, he wants me to picture myself at my *best*. I am to contemplate the mystery of my identity as a daughter of God in Christ, who gave his followers the Beatitudes as a "plan of holiness."[4]

In instructing us to put our own face on the Beatitudes, Francis provides a creative counterpoint to the *Catechism*, which says "the Beatitudes depict the countenance of Jesus Christ and portray his charity" (CCC 1717). We discover our identity in the Beatitudes because they bring us to contemplate the face of Jesus.

I am reminded of one of Francis's favorite verbal images: through faith, our faces become as a mirror reflecting the face of Christ. In *Lumen fidei*, he draws out the implications of this image as it appears in a passage from St. Paul: "God . . . has shone in our hearts to give the light of the knowledge of the glory of God in the face of Christ" (2 Cor 4:6, RSV). "The light of Christ shines, as in a mirror, upon the face of Christians," Francis says. "As it spreads, it comes down to us, so that we too can share in that vision and reflect that light to others, in the same way that, in the Easter liturgy, the light of the paschal candle lights countless other candles."[5]

For Francis, then, we receive our identity as Christians through encountering the light of Christ—the faith passed down through the Church—just as the candle we hold at the Easter Vigil Mass receives its flame through encountering the flame passed down from the paschal candle.

## ENCOUNTERING CHRIST THROUGH HIS WOUNDS

By employing the symbolism of the paschal candle in his discussion of Christian identity, Francis invites an additional layer of symbolism, one that has special meaning for those who have suffered any kind of wound.

The paschal candle is lit during the first part of the Easter Vigil liturgy to symbolize (in the words of the *Roman Missal*) "the light of Christ rising in glory" that "[dispels] the darkness of our hearts and minds." Just prior to lighting the candle, the priest inserts five grains of incense into the candle in the form of a cross, symbolizing the wounds of Christ. As he sinks the grains into the wax, he prays, "By his holy and glorious wounds, may Christ the Lord guard us and protect us."

So we see that it is only after these wounds are called to memory that the light of the risen Christ, symbolized by the ignited candle, shines forth and spreads its glow to every candle in the church. Francis says, "His glorious wounds are a scandal for faith but also the proof of faith."[6] The light of faith—the *lumen fidei* that shines upon us and gives us our identity as Christians—is the light of Christ precisely as *wounded*. A Scholastic theologian such as Thomas Aquinas might say that the light of Christ comes to us under the "species" of Christ's woundedness—and Aquinas does in fact say something very much like that in his *Summa theologiae*. He says, "The Eucharist is the sacrament of Christ's Passion according as a man is made perfect in union with *Christum passum*"—Christ who suffered.[7]

This, then, is the Christ we encounter and imitate through the Beatitudes: Christ who poured himself out for us upon the Cross, and who now, even in heaven, pours himself out for us through his "holy and glorious wounds." In emptying himself, he gives us the model for the first of the Beatitudes, the one from which all the others proceed: "Blessed are the poor in spirit, for theirs is the kingdom of heaven." Jesus became poor for our sake, so that we might become rich (2 Cor 8:9). He suffered for us as an example so that we might follow in his steps (1 Pt 2:21). And the Beatitudes comprise the ladder by which we ascend to heaven.

Among the rungs of this ladder, there is one Beatitude that the *Catechism* presents as holding unique significance for our growth in love of God and neighbor: "Blessed are the pure in heart, for they shall see God." In order to truly get inside this, the sixth beatitude, we have to first go deeper into the beatitude of the poor in spirit. For those two beatitudes are intimately connected, and Pope Francis shows us where to find the connections.

## POVERTY OF SPIRIT: LIVING OUT YOUR BAPTISM

As we trace the connections that Francis indicates between poverty of spirit and purity in heart, two words show themselves to be very important to understanding how the pope associates those Beatitudes. The words are "love" and "flesh."

Let's start with "love." Francis would have us ponder, "What is this poverty by which Christ frees us and enriches us?" The answer, he says, is that Christ's poverty "is his way of loving us, his way of being our neighbor."[8] And what is Jesus' way of loving us? It is to insert us into his relationship with the Father. Francis says, "When Jesus asks us to take up his 'yoke which is easy,' he asks us to be enriched by his 'poverty which is rich' and his 'richness which is poor,' to share his filial and fraternal Spirit, to become sons and daughters in the Son, brothers and sisters in the firstborn brother."[9]

The blessing of the poor in spirit, then, is the blessing of those who live out the baptismal relationship that they have with God and with one another. In this way, Francis says, it is Christ's poverty that saves us. "In every time and place God continues to save mankind and the world through the poverty of Christ, who makes himself poor in the sacraments, in his word and in his Church, which is a people of the poor."[10]

This brings us to the other word that is important for Francis's understanding of the connection between poverty of spirit and purity of heart: "flesh." We have seen that our encounter with the light of Christ is an encounter with he who bears "glorious wounds." Those glorious wounds manifest Christ's poverty of spirit, the poverty that saves us by bringing us into the family of God. We manifest *our* poverty of spirit by acting as children of our heavenly Father, sharing his love—and the way we do this, Francis says, is by touching "the wounded flesh of Jesus."[11]

"This is our poverty," he insists, "the poverty of the flesh of Christ, the poverty that the Son of God brought us with His Incarnation. A poor Church for the poor begins by going to the flesh of Christ. If we go to the flesh of Christ, we begin to understand something, to understand what this poverty is, the poverty of the Lord."[12]

In this light, our poverty of spirit takes on a profoundly eucharistic dimension. Jesus, in the Eucharist, touches us with his wounded flesh so that we might recognize his wounded flesh in others and reach out to them in love. Francis writes in *Lumen fidei*, "By his taking flesh and coming among us, Jesus has touched us, and through the sacraments he continues to touch us even today; transforming our hearts, he unceasingly enables us to acknowledge and acclaim him as the Son of God."[13]

## PURITY OF HEART: BUILDING UP YOUR CAPACITY FOR GOD

With those words of Francis, we now begin to see the connection between poverty of spirit and purity of heart. If poverty of spirit is the fruit of our initial encounter with Jesus' love, purity of heart is the fruit of that same encounter extended through time, as divine grace operates within us to affect our continued transformation.

To understand the meaning of purity of heart, Francis says, "we need to appreciate the biblical meaning of the word heart."[14] He explains, "In Hebrew thought, the heart is the center of the emotions, thoughts, and intentions of the human person. Since the Bible teaches us that God does not look to appearances, but to the heart . . . , we can also say that it is from the heart that we see God. This is because the heart is really the human being in his or her totality as a unity of body and soul, in his or her [capacity] to love and to be loved."[15]

Purity of heart builds up our *capax Dei*—the God-shaped vacuum in our heart. We could even say, in the words of St. Augustine, that it *stretches* the heart. Augustine notes, "What you desire, . . . you don't yet see. But by desiring you are made large enough, so that, when there comes what you should see, you may be filled. . . . This is how God stretches our desire through delay, stretches our soul through desire, and makes it large enough by stretching it."[16]

Poverty of spirit for Francis, then, unites us with Jesus' saving love, while purity of heart expands our heart so that we may become conduits of that same love. In that light, purity of heart can be seen as our participation in the love that saves us. The suffering we undergo in being purified is our *com*-passion in Christ's passion. Blessed John Henry Newman says, "Purity prepares the soul for love, and love confirms the soul in purity. The flame of love will not be bright unless the substance which feeds it be pure and unadulterate; and the most dazzling purity is but as iciness and desolation unless it draws its life from fervent love."[17]

## A WOMAN OF THE BEATITUDES

Francis observes that such fervent love was the hallmark of the woman who lived the Beatitudes so perfectly that she was assumed into heaven. "The Mother of the Crucified and Risen One has entered the sanctuary of divine mercy because she participated intimately in the mystery of His love."[18] That is why Mary is our model for purity of heart, even though she herself, being preserved from sin, was never in need of purification. She suffered with Jesus, and, when her earthly life was completed, she rose with him (Rom 8:17, 2 Tm 2:12).

Yet, Mary is far more than a mere example for us to follow. Through her *fiat*—her joyful "yes" at the annunciation (Lk 1:38)—she is also our Mother and guide. "Mary's 'yes,' already perfect from the start, grew until the hour of the Cross," Francis says. "There, her motherhood opened to embrace every one of us, our lives, so as to guide us to her Son."[19]

"We can ask ourselves a question," Francis adds. "Do we allow ourselves to be illumined by the faith of Mary, who is our Mother? Or do we think of her as distant, as someone too different from us?"[20]

Mary is not a plaster saint. Francis urges us to think of her as a real woman, alive in heaven, ready to aid us through the grace she has received through her unique relationship with God. "Completely transfigured, she now lives with Jesus. She treasures the entire life of Jesus in her heart, and now understands the meaning of all things. Hence, we can ask her to enable us to look at this world with eyes of wisdom."[21]

## PRAYING FOR PURITY

I long to have those "eyes of wisdom" so I might gain the purity of heart that enabled Mary to begin enjoying the life of heaven while still on earth. So I ask Mary's help in many different ways.

Most of the means I use to approach Mary are devotional practices that every Catholic knows, such as the Rosary and daily Mass (which for me has proven to be a truly life-changing habit). Some are practices I learned through the Dominican Order's Angelic Warfare Confraternity (www.angelicwarfareconfraternity.org), a fellowship of men and women who unite themselves in prayer to live chastely in imitation of Mary and St. Thomas Aquinas. But there is one lesser-known Marian devotion that I have found particularly helpful for developing purity of heart: the Seven Sorrows.

Also known by its Latin name *Via Matris* ("Way of the Mother"), the Seven Sorrows devotion consists of seven "stations"—painful events in Mary's life that are caused by, or point to, the rejection of her Son. There are various ways of praying the devotion; mine is to say a Hail Mary for each sorrow:

1. The prophecy of Simeon (Lk 2:34–35)

2. The flight into Egypt (Mt 2:13–14)

3. The three days' loss of the Child Jesus (Lk 3:43–45)

4. The meeting of Jesus and Mary on the Way of the Cross

5. The Crucifixion

6. The taking down of Jesus' body from the Cross

7. The burial of Jesus

This devotion first attracted me because it is about facing trauma in the company of Mary and Jesus. Mary, through her lifetime of compassion, modeled the compassion through which I too am called to unite my wounded heart to the wounded and glorified heart of Jesus. In that light, I found the prayer to be a powerful tool for healing of memories.

But I have since discovered that the Seven Sorrows devotion can do more than heal my memories. It can also help me grow in grace, if I pray it for the specific intention of purity of heart. I do this by meditating upon each sorrow for healing from the temptation to one of the seven deadly sins—the sins that traditionally "are called 'capital' because they engender other sins, other vices" (CCC 1866). As I make the contemplation, I look to Mary for guidance to obtain the virtue that will enable me to conquer each of my personal evils.

Pray the Seven Sorrows with me:

1. **The prophecy of Simeon:** We pray for healing from the temptation to envy.

Envy is sorrow over another person's good. When Mary heard Simeon say that, because of Jesus, a sword would pierce her own soul (Lk 2:35, RSV), she experienced the opposite of envy. She felt sorrow at the evil that would befall her Son—so much so that she wished, if it were possible, that she could suffer the evil in his place. *Mary, pray that I may expand my heart so that I may "rejoice with those who rejoice [and] weep with those who weep"* (Rom 12:15).

2. **The flight into Egypt:** We pray for healing from the temptation to sloth.

Mary and Joseph did not delay in obeying the angel's instruction to leave their home and relatives to become exiles in a foreign land. They were swift to do everything God called them to do, to the sacrifice of their personal comfort, for the love of Jesus. *Mary, pray that I may persevere in running the race before me, keeping my eyes fixed on Jesus* (Heb 12:1–2).

3. **The three days' loss of the Child Jesus:** We pray for healing from the temptation to anger.

When Mary and Joseph found their twelve-year-old Son in the Temple after searching for him for three days, it would have been natural for them to be angry with him for causing them such distress. But Mary, although making it clear to Jesus that she and Joseph were distressed, spoke to him only with the purest love (Lk 2:48). *Mary, show me how to bear the love that is patient and kind, not quick-tempered, not brooding over injury* (1 Cor 13:4–5).

**4. The meeting of Jesus and Mary on the Way of the Cross:** We pray for healing from the temptation to gluttony.

Mary hungered to see Jesus' face one last time. She gazed at him knowing he was the Way, the Truth, and the Life. To live in his love was the fulfillment of all her desire. *Mary, pray that I may have the blessing of those "who hunger and thirst for righteousness, for they will be satisfied"* (Mt 5:6).

**5. The Crucifixion:** We pray for healing from the temptation to lust.

Mary witnessed Jesus, her own flesh and blood, endure nails in his flesh so that he might take away the sins of the world—including the sins of the flesh. *Blessed Mother, pray that my sinful desires may be crucified with Christ, so that I may glorify God in my body* (Gal 2:19, 1 Cor 6:20).

**6. The taking down of Jesus' body from the Cross:** We pray for healing from the temptation to pride.

Mary could not take pride in her immaculate conception. She had nothing that she had not received. What overwhelming gratitude she must have felt as she witnessed her Son having completed his sacrifice, realizing that her own freedom from sin was granted by God by virtue of the foreseen merits that Jesus would win for the human race (CCC 491). *Mary, pray that I may have the blessing of the poor in spirit, so that I may attain the kingdom of heaven* (Mt 5:3).

7. **The burial of Jesus:** We pray for healing from the temptation to covetousness.

Mary witnessed Jesus' burial in a tomb acquired by a rich man (Jn 19:38)—a strange irony, since neither she nor Jesus had ever sought material wealth. Jesus was, like his heavenly Father, "rich in mercy, because of the great love he had for us" (Eph 2:4), while Mary stored up treasures not on earth but in heaven (Mt 6:19–20). *Mary, pray that my treasures will be where yours are, so that my heart will be there too* (Mt 6:21).

We end our petitions for purity of heart by taking these words of Pope Francis to prayer: "The joy of the Gospel arises from a heart which, in its poverty, rejoices and marvels at the works of God, like the heart of Our Lady, whom all generations call 'blessed.' May Mary, Mother of the poor and Star of the new evangelization help us to live the Gospel, to embody the Beatitudes in our lives, and to have the courage always to be happy."[22]

# 5

# AND SURRENDER IT WHOLLY TO BE GOVERNED BY YOUR WILL

## *Praying with Courage*

IIIIIIIIIIIIIIIIIIIIIIIIIIIIIIIIIIIIIIIIIIIIIIIIIIIIIIIIIIIIIIIIIIIIIIIII

When Jorge Bergoglio, as a Jesuit novice, made his first Long Retreat, one instruction that comes up several times during the Spiritual Exercises made a deep impression upon him: "I will ask for the grace I desire." The instruction reflects how Ignatius wanted the Jesuits to have the courage to lay out their desires before God. For Ignatius, as for St. Paul, it is God's own grace that enables us to desire what he wills for us (Phil 2:13).

That same courage that Ignatius sought of his companions is what Francis now seeks from of all the faithful. He not only says "prayer must be courageous"[1] but even

goes so far as to assert that "prayer that is not courageous is not real prayer."[2] While we usually associate the
courage of the faithful with those who have missionary
zeal, "there is also courage in standing before the Lord
. . . in going bravely to the Lord to ask him things. . . . It
is tiring, true, but this is prayer. This is what receiving a
grace from God is."[3]

## IGNATIUS'S SPIRITUAL BREAKTHROUGH

Ignatius of Loyola, as a young soldier, was admired by his
peers for his great courage, but he was loath to expend
his energies in prayer. Instead, as we saw in chapter 1,
he was by his own account consumed with "a vain and
overpowering desire to gain renown."[4]

In 1521, when Ignatius was about twenty-nine years
old,[5] one of his legs was shattered by a cannonball during
battle. A field doctor attempted to set the leg, but the
bones did not heal properly. Once Ignatius was trans-
ported home to Loyola Castle, his wealthy family called
in experts who determined it was necessary to break the
bones again and reset them. Owing to the primitive state
of medicine of the time, he endured the procedure with
no anesthesia.

The second procedure was successful: Ignatius's leg
healed to the extent that he could walk again. But Ignatius was not satisfied, for the bones below the knee were
set awkwardly, so that his leg was shortened and there
was an unsightly bump. In his autobiography (which

is written in the third person, as he narrated it to his secretary), he tells how his vanity drove him to drastic measures: "Because he was determined to make a way for himself in the world, he could not tolerate such ugliness and thought [the bump] marred his appearance. Thus he instructed the surgeons to remove it, if possible. They told him that it could certainly be sawn away, but the pain would be greater than any he had suffered up to now. . . . Nevertheless, he was determined to endure this martyrdom to satisfy his personal taste."[6]

Note the self-mockery in Ignatius's description of his willingness to undergo "martyrdom" for the god of his personal vanity. He is setting the stage for the moment when God would use his infirmity as a means of drawing him to sanctity.

That moment came as Ignatius was recovering from the procedure. Being confined to bed, he asked his sister Magdalena, the lady of the castle, to bring him some books to read. He was hoping for "books of worldly fiction, commonly called chivalrous romances"—tales of knights in armor doing brave deeds to win the esteem of beautiful ladies.[7] But all Magdalena could offer him was Christian literature—a book on the life of Christ, and another on the lives of the saints.

Ignatius found himself reading the Christian books often and, perhaps to his surprise, growing fond of them. Even so, his imagination remained full of the fantasies he had fostered through filling his mind with tales of chivalry: "Of the many idle things that came to him, one took such a hold on his heart that, without his realizing it, it engrossed him for two or three hours at a time. He dreamed what he would achieve in the service of a certain lady."[8]

His romantic fantasies were quite detailed: he tells us he imagined his journey to the country where this very high-born lady lived, the words he would say to her, and the knightly deeds he would accomplish to impress her. But, by God's grace, those thoughts were not the only ones that entered his mind as he lay on his sickbed. "While reading the life of our Lord and those of the saints, he used to pause and meditate, reasoning within himself: 'What if I were to do what St. Francis did, or what St. Dominic did?'"[9]

Just as Ignatius's worldly imaginings centered on doing magnificent things in the service of a lady, so too his meditations inspired by the saints led him to envision himself accomplishing difficult deeds in the service of God. He thought of "going barefoot to Jerusalem and eating nothing but herbs, and . . . imitating the saints in all the austerities they practiced."[10] If St. Francis or St. Dominic could do it, then he could do it—in fact, he felt, he *had* to do it.

Such holy thoughts would occupy Ignatius's mind for long periods, but eventually he would get distracted and return to worldly fantasies. One day, however, he paused to reflect upon where his thoughts were taking him. He noticed that when he immersed himself in fantasies of doing heroic knightly deeds for a royal lady, "he found much delight; but, after growing weary and dismissing them, he found that he was dry and unhappy."[11] But when he thought of imitating the radical sacrifices of the saints, "he not only found consolation in these thoughts, but even after they left him he remained happy and joyful."[12]

Ignatius writes that, as he contemplated how "some thoughts left him sad while others made him happy, . . . little by little he came to perceive the different spirits that were moving him; one coming from the devil, the other coming from God."[13]

That realization marked the beginning of Ignatius's reflections upon discernment of spirits, gathering insights that would eventually bear great fruit as he composed his Spiritual Exercises. As Pope Francis has noted, discernment of spirits became for the saint "an instrument of struggle in order to know the Lord and follow him more closely."[14]

## AGERE CONTRA: A TOOL FOR COUNTERING TEMPTATION

An expert on Ignatius writes that, in the saint's terminology, "to discern is to see deeply with a view to recognizing and distinguishing."[15] In my own life, as a PTSD sufferer, I have found Ignatian discernment extraordinarily helpful. It enables me to cope at times when something happens that triggers a memory of past pain.

Ignatian discernment is a field all its own, and there are many good books for those interested in studying it in depth.[16] But the aspect of it that has helped me the most is one that is not often treated at length in

Ignatian literature, and I think it should be. It's the manner in which Ignatius approaches an ancient principle of combating temptation. The principle is known as *agere contra*, Latin for "to act against." It means responding to temptation by aggressively doing the opposite of what the evil spirit—or our own less-than-godly desires— would have us do.[17]

When Ignatius counsels agere contra, he often does so to restore balance to retreatants who are troubled by psychological pain, as in the section of the Spiritual Exercises concerning "scruples and the temptations of our enemy."[18] Giving guidance for those afflicted with scrupulosity[19]—an obsessive fear of committing sin that can lead its victims to despair of God's mercy—the saint writes, "A soul that wishes to make progress in the spiritual life must always act in a manner contrary to that of the enemy. If the enemy seeks to make the conscience lax, one must endeavor to make it more sensitive. If the enemy strives to make the conscience delicate with a view to leading it to excess, the soul must endeavor to establish itself firmly in a moderate course so that in all things it may preserve itself in peace."[20]

Ignatius was able to bring particular gentleness and wisdom to the problem of scrupulosity, because he knew what it was like, having suffered terribly from it during the months following his conversion experience. In 1522, while living at a Dominican monastery in Manresa, Spain, he was continually tormented with the thought that he had failed to confess certain past sins, or had not confessed them as well as he should have.

His autobiography tells of a time when his anxious fears drove him to the brink of suicide: "Taken up with these thoughts, he was many times vehemently tempted to throw himself into a deep hole in his room, which was near the place where he used to pray. But realizing that it was a sin to kill oneself, he again cried out: 'Lord, I will do nothing to offend you.' He many times repeated these words as well as the former ones."[21]

Although the saint at that time still had much to learn in the spiritual life, his desperate cry to the Lord represents the beginnings of the insights that would lead him to greatness. He understood that temptations could be successively countered only by centering one's thoughts upon Christ rather than upon self.

## PSYCHOLOGICAL HEALING AND SPIRITUAL COMBAT

You don't have to be Catholic to benefit from the psychology behind *agere contra*. In the bestselling *Man's Search for Meaning*, Jewish psychiatrist Viktor Frankl, the survivor of the Auschwitz death camp who developed the form of counseling known as logotherapy, describes using a similar approach with great success.

Frankl calls his approach "paradoxical intention." In it, he writes, "The phobic patient is invited to intend, even if only for a moment, precisely that which he fears."[22]

In one case, a young doctor came to Frankl seeking to overcome his fear of sweating. "Whenever he expected an outbreak of perspiration, this anticipatory anxiety was enough to precipitate excessive sweating." The psychiatrist's response was to instruct the patient that, the next time he expected such an outbreak, he should "resolve deliberately to show people how much he could sweat."[23]

"A week later," Frankl writes, "[the patient] returned to report that whenever he met anyone who triggered his anticipatory anxiety, he said to himself, 'I only sweated out a quart before, but now I am going to pour at least ten quarts!' The result was that, after suffering from his phobia for four years, he was able, after a single session, to free himself permanently of it within one week."[24]

What exactly took place in this psychiatrist/patient interaction? As I see it, the patient entered Frankl's office carrying the unhealthy mental intention, "I am going to sweat; therefore, I am fearful."

Note that the intention has two parts. The first—the certainty of sweating—is beyond the patient's control. It is not in a human being's power to turn off sweat glands at will. But the second part of the intention *is* within the patient's control. If sweating is inevitable, he can choose how he will accept it—either with fear or with confident determination.

Frankl's genius is in advising the patient to take the part of the patient's unhealthy intention that he can control and flip it on its head so that fear can no longer win the day. His recommendation, if written as an intention, would be, "I am going to sweat; therefore I will put my best effort into it—for if I'm going to be a sweaty mess, I might as well be a *hardworking* sweaty mess."

Although paradoxical intention operates similarly to agere contra, there is a key difference: paradoxical intention is a tool for psychological healing, but agere contra is a weapon of spiritual combat. Ignatius makes this abundantly clear in his exercises: it is to be employed against temptations sent by "the enemy"—Ignatius's preferred term for the devil—that threaten to impede one's growth in grace.

Witness, for example, the advice Ignatius gives to those who, suffering desolation (darkness of soul), are tempted to shorten the contemplative exercises so that they pray for less than the required hour. "In order to fight against the desolation and conquer the temptation," Ignatius writes, "the [retreatant] must always remain in the exercise a little more than the full hour. Thus he will accustom himself not only to resist the enemy, but even to overthrow him."

In this example given by Ignatius, the retreatant's point of spiritual vulnerability is his or her faulty mental intention, which could be summarized, "I am incapable of praying properly; therefore I will shorten my prayer time."

As with the example from Frankl, the first part of that intention is beyond the retreatant's control. Ignatius tells us that in cases of desolation, "God has left [the retreatant] to his natural powers to resist the different agitations and temptations of the enemy in order to try him." Although the retreatant who perseveres in patience still has sufficient grace to be saved, it is not in his or her power to return to a state of consolation. The power to restore him belongs to God alone.[25]

Therefore, Ignatius advises the retreatant to put all his effort into accomplishing that which *is* under his control. His recommendation, if written as an intention, would be, "I am incapable of praying properly; therefore, I will *lengthen* my prayer time—because it is better to try and fail at praying, than not to try at all."

## THE JESUS PRAYER: HEALING OIL FOR THE SOUL

I have cited an example of agere contra involving prayer because I have found that, in my own journey to healing in Christ, agere contra has helped me the most by strengthening my prayer life. It especially helped me when I employed it to help me pray a prayer I had long resisted: the Jesus Prayer.

The Jesus Prayer is adapted from the repentant cry of the publican in Luke 18:13. Of its many forms, the most popular one is: "Lord Jesus Christ, Son of God, have mercy on me, a sinner." Praying it in any of its variations is a means of fulfilling the scriptural exhortation to "pray without ceasing" (1 Thes 5:17).

Pope Francis speaks with reverence of a man who worked in the diocesan curia of Buenos Aires, a father of eight, who prayed the Jesus Prayer in its simplest form—just repeating the Holy Name: "Before going out, before going to do any of the things he had to do, he would whisper to himself: 'Jesus!' I once asked him, 'Why do you keep saying Jesus?' 'When I say Jesus,' this humble man answered me, 'I feel strong, I feel able to work because I know he is beside me, that he is preserving me.'"[26]

This man, the pope adds, "had not studied theology. He had only the grace of Baptism and the power of the Spirit. His witness did so much good for me. The name of Jesus. There is no other name."[27]

The person who taught me the value of incorporating the Jesus Prayer into my prayer life was my friend Jeffry Hendrix, who had been a United Methodist pastor before coming home to the Catholic Church.

Jeffry's life underwent a traumatic upheaval in 2008 when he was diagnosed with kidney cancer. While undergoing treatment, he was moved to write a book to help others who were likewise finding themselves forced to face their own mortality: *A Little Guide for Your Last Days*.

It was then, after I offered to proofread Jeffry's manuscript, that I discovered how the Jesus Prayer helped him find spiritual healing. He suggested it to readers as a tool for overcoming personal resentment, teaching them a method that had worked wonders in his own life. As I reread his words now, I realize for the first time that they are an application of *agere contra*:

> Now, here is my recommendation. After crossing yourself—the timeless gesture of placing yourself under the jurisdiction of the Most Holy Trinity—begin by praying the Jesus Prayer with you in the "me" place of the

> prayer. Then, insert each of your loved ones
> in turn. ("Lord Jesus Christ, Son of God, have
> mercy on [name], a sinner.") Then and only
> then, insert the name of the one who you feel
> has wronged you, hurt you, done damage to
> you, neglected you. Whatever.
>
> You are thus fulfilling Our Lord's injunc-
> tion to forgive your "enemy" and, at the same
> time, shielding yourself from the bitter res-
> idue of resentment that can rot your heart
> and soul.[28]

We could say that, in essence, Jeffry is recommending
the prayer for those of us who suffer from a harmful
mental intention, one which runs like this: "[Name] is a
sinner; therefore I do not believe [name] deserves God's
mercy."

As with our other examples of agere contra, the first
part of the intention can't be changed. If someone has
sinned against us, even if he or she repents, the evil of the
past can't be erased. But the second part *is* within our
power to change, and that is where Jeffry would have us
alter our intention. Under his guidance, if we pray the
Jesus Prayer first for ourselves, then for each of our loved
ones, and finally for that person, our intention effectively
becomes: "[Name] is a sinner; I too am a sinner, therefore
I believe [name] deserves the same mercy that has been
shown me."

Praying in the manner Jeffry recommends is a true
formula for holiness. It was my blessing, as Jeffry's friend,
to see him grow in such holiness, finding ever-greater

spiritual healing until he passed away in 2011 at the age of fifty-six. Eight days before his death, he shared with me in an e-mail the prayer that was in his heart: "I offer up all the blessings of my life, and look forward, ever forward to serving even more faithfully."

As I contemplate how the Jesus Prayer led Jeffry to overcome spiritual obstacles, I am reminded of an insight of Albert S. Rossi, an Eastern Orthodox psychologist, on the origin of the word *eleison*, which is Greek for "mercy."

"*Eleison*," Rossi writes, "has the same root as *elaion*, which means olive and olive oil. In the Middle East, olive oil provides physical healing for many sicknesses. . . . 'Have mercy' means to have 'healing oil' on my soul." In this way, "the Jesus Prayer functions as therapy, much like healing oil, transforming our personality from overstrain to joy, and by continuing to pray, these changes become permanent."[29]

## FROM MISERY TO MERCY

As I said, for a long time I resisted praying the Jesus Prayer—and this despite my admiration of Jeffry. I didn't pray it because, frankly, it made me uncomfortable.

To my mind, praying over and over, "Lord Jesus Christ, Son of God, have mercy on me, a sinner," seemed like a surefire way to spend one's day in self-pity: "Look at poor itsy-bitsy me, having to tell God ten thousand times how miserable I am."

Granted, many a sinner had become a saint through praying the Jesus Prayer. I knew that. But I couldn't get over the feeling that praying it would feel humiliating, if not downright depressing. It was fine for the confessional; perhaps, in saying it there, I might even bring a sigh of relief to my confessor, as it shaves about forty-five seconds off the time it takes to make the standard act of contrition. But for everyday life? Not a chance.

All that changed in the autumn of 2012 when, as a graduate student living in Washington, DC, I was hit hard with an unnerving flare-up of PTSD.

I remember that the episode seemed to come on suddenly, although it was most likely triggered by a combination of stressful situations in my daily life. In any case, it took me by surprise, since I had been managing well for some time.

Unfortunately, as I wrote in chapter 3, once a PTSD episode begins, and the sufferer's body becomes awash in stress hormones, the disorder's effects can't simply be wished away by thinking good thoughts. This particular episode was the longest one I had suffered in years. All in all, it lasted about two weeks, though it seemed longer because, as I was in the midst of it, I could not see any end in sight. I knew only that I was constantly on edge, constantly teary, and—most distressingly—had to actively fight impulses to harm myself.

The self-destructive impulses crossed my mind like brief flashes. They seemed to come from a place where I had stored pent-up anger—a feeling for which I had no legitimate outlet for as a child, being powerless to demand protection. Knowing that the impulses did not reflect my true desires, I would quickly put them out of my thoughts, but they frightened me nonetheless.[30]

I write in *My Peace I Give You* about how, during an attack of PTSD, it is possible to find grace and healing through bringing the embodied effects of past traumas into union with Jesus' passion. Doing so, however, requires making a constant effort in prayer to bring all one's thoughts and affections in line with those of the Sacred Heart of Jesus. I knew, as I suffered through this episode, that I had to make such an effort—and, to my surprise, the means that came to me was the Jesus Prayer.

The image remains clear in my mind: I can see myself leaving school at the end of the day, making the six-minute walk toward the Metro station as my throat choked up with stress. The leaves on the trees lining the sidewalks were tinged with orange and red. An unmuffled sport-utility vehicle passed by me quickly, and I turned to see the source of the noise; as I did, the thought crossed my mind, *I could have jumped in front of that car and it would all have been over.*

Suddenly, seemingly without deliberation, I found myself responding to the frightening impulse with a prayer: "Lord Jesus Christ, Son of God, have mercy on me, a sinner." I said it again. And again. And, as I did, something began to happen.

The prayer felt humiliating—but not in the way that I had feared it would. As I continued to pray it, I realized that the feeling I had wasn't that of wallowing. The prayer was not leading me to self-pity. It was rather opening my heart to the purifying love of God.

Those words, "Lord Jesus Christ, Son of God, have mercy on me, a sinner," tore into me like steel wool, reaching into my depths and cleaning out the spiritual rust—what Jeffry had called "the bitter residue of resentment that can rot your heart and soul."[31]

I could feel that my eyes were wet. That in itself was not unusual; I had been crying every day for the past week. But what was unusual was that the tears no longer felt toxic. They felt purifying, the way they do when my eyes water to cleanse themselves in the presence of smoke. I felt as though the white heat of divine love was burning away the feelings of anger that had isolated me in my pain.

It had taken courage for me to pray the Jesus Prayer. But through it I learned, as Pope Francis says, that "when we pray courageously, the Lord not only gives us grace; he gives us his very self in the grace."[32]

As I approached the stairs leading down into the darkness of the Metro station, I did not know how much longer the PTSD episode would endure. But I did know one thing that I did not know six minutes earlier, before I began to pray the Jesus Prayer. I knew—not just in my mind but in my heart—that I was not alone. I had asked for a grace, the grace of Jesus' presence in my suffering, and had received it.

"Certain realities of life," Pope Francis says, "are seen only with eyes that are cleansed by tears."[33]

## LEARNING HOW TO ASK

Francis once reflected upon a prayer used in Catholic liturgy that petitions the Lord to "give what prayer does not dare to ask":[34] "What is [it] that we don't know how to ask for? For him! We ask for a grace, but we do not know how to say to him: come and bring it to me."[35]

And so, he says, we need to learn how to courageously ask the Lord for the grace we seek. We do this, he says, by giving him praise for his gifts "and [appealing to him] who is so merciful, so good, to help us."[36]

That is why Francis recommends we pray Psalm 103 each day, for through it "we learn the things we must say to the Lord when we request a grace."[37] Pray the beginning of it with me:

> Bless the LORD, my soul;
> all my being, bless his holy name!
> Bless the LORD, my soul;
> and do not forget all his gifts,
> Who pardons all your sins,
> and heals all your ills,
> Who redeems your life from the pit,
> and crowns you with mercy and
>     compassion.

# 6

# GIVE ME ONLY YOUR LOVE AND YOUR GRACE

*Expanding Your Heart through Prayer*

||||||||||||||||||||||||||||||||||||||||||||||||||||||||||||||||||||||

One day in late 1969, Jorge Mario Bergoglio wrote on a scrap of paper, "I believe in my history, which was infused with the loving gaze of God, who, on a spring day . . . , crossed my path and invited me to follow him."

The words formed part of a personal creed that the thirty-three-year-old Jesuit wrote shortly before his priestly ordination, during what he would later say was a time of "great spiritual intensity" for him. As he jotted down his reflections on the workings of grace in his life and his response to them, he was filled with gratitude for the day he heard the call to the priesthood.

That day—September 21, 1953—was still fresh in Francis's mind when, two months into his pontificate, on

the eve of Pentecost, he described his powerful "experience of encounter" with the Lord to an audience in St.
Peter's Square:

> I was almost seventeen. It was "Students'
> Day," for us [in Buenos Aires] the first day
> of spring—for you the first day of autumn.
> Before going to the celebration, I passed
> through the parish I normally attended, I
> found a priest that I did not know, and I felt
> the need to go to confession.
>
> For me this was an experience of encoun-
> ter: I found that someone was waiting for me.
> Yet I do not know what happened, I can't
> remember, I do not know why that particu-
> lar priest was there whom I did not know, or
> why I felt this desire to confess, but the truth
> is that someone was waiting for me. He had
> been waiting for me for some time.
>
> After making my confession I felt some-
> thing had changed. I was not the same. I had
> heard something like a voice, or a call. I was
> convinced that I should become a priest.[1]

The fact that September 21 is the feast of St. Matthew, the tax collector who was called by Christ, was not
lost on the young Francis. As an archbishop, he told his
biographers that he was "always very moved"[2] by a line
in the breviary (the book containing the Liturgy of the
Hours that priests are required to pray daily)[3] from St.
Bede that described the way Jesus gazed upon Matthew.

"Jesus saw a publican," Bede writes, "and since
he looked at him with feelings of love and chose

him"—*miserando atque eligendo,* in the original Latin—"he said to him, 'Follow me.'"[4]

Francis so identified with that passage that he made *miserando atque eligendo* his episcopal motto.[5] He would later explain to an interviewer why he retained the motto as pope: "I am a sinner whom the Lord has looked upon. I am one who is looked upon by the Lord. I always felt my motto was very true for me."[6]

## SALVATION: THE MEETING WHERE GOD WORKS FIRST

The memory of his vocational call was the lens through which Francis came to see God as being always *primerea* —the playful term we noted in chapter 1, which he uses to describe how "the Lord always gets there before us."[7] As he pursued his theology studies, that same memory would influence his understanding of Augustine, enabling him to gain deep personal insight into the saint's teachings on grace.

In an essay written while he was a cardinal, Francis seems to draw upon his personal experience as he comments upon a passage where Augustine describes the way Jesus gazed upon Zacchaeus—who, like St. Matthew, was a tax collector (Lk 19:1–10). Augustine wrote that as Zacchaeus, having climbed a sycamore tree, attempted to get a view of Jesus, "the Lord looked at Zacchaeus himself. He was seen, and saw."

Francis reflects,

Some believe that faith and salvation come
with our effort to look for, to seek the Lord.
Whereas it's the opposite: you are saved when
the Lord looks for you, when He looks at you
and you let yourself be looked at and sought
for. The Lord will look for you first. And when
you find him, you understand that he was
waiting there looking at you, He was expecting you from beforehand.

That is salvation: He loves you beforehand. And you let yourself be loved. Salvation is precisely this meeting where he works
first. If this meeting does not take place, we
are not saved.[8]

"He loves you beforehand. And you let yourself
be loved." It seems to me that those beautiful words
not only encapsulate Augustine's message but also tie
together the experiences of St. Matthew, Zacchaeus, and
the young Francis with that of St. Ignatius of Loyola.

Let us take a deeper look at the connection. Recall
how, as we saw in chapter 1, Ignatius in his Suscipe
prayer offers God his entire liberty, his memory, his
understanding, and his whole will—in a word, himself.
In exchange, he asks, "Give me only your love and your
grace." He is able to make his self-offering to God only
because God, in a free and generous gift of love, has
already given him everything he has; as we read in that
same prayer, "All that I am and all that I possess you
have given me: I surrender it all to you to be disposed of
according to your will."

Like Matthew, Zacchaeus, and Francis, Ignatius knows
God has loved him beforehand. In making his Suscipe
prayer, he makes his free choice to let himself be loved.

But there is more, for Ignatius's choice to let himself be loved is not just a one-time act. He intends his
Suscipe prayer as a complete gift of self; its message
becomes part of his makeup. As he prays it in response to
the love of Jesus, who is "the Word" (*logos*, in Greek), the
act of praying brings him and God into dialogue (from
the Greek *dia-logos*).

This dialogue into which Ignatius enters through
praying the Suscipe (and which he invites us to enter
as well) is meant to be ongoing—continuing throughout Ignatius's earthly life, and on into eternity. Francis
writes in *Lumen fidei* that "[God] is an eternal dialogue
of communion"; he allows us "to enter into dialogue with
[him], to be embraced by his mercy and then to bring
that mercy to others."[9]

It is a dialogue characterized by intimacy, for God
"has chosen us one by one. He has given us a name. And
he looks upon us. There is a dialogue, because this is the
way the Lord loves."[10]

This indeed is the way the Lord loves. God, who is
love (1 Jn 4:8), loves us first, enabling us to let ourselves
be loved. Then he continues to speak to us through his
love, so that we might always return to him a greater gift
than that which we first received.

What is more, as we enter more deeply into this
dialogue, allowing ourselves to be ever more deeply
"embraced by his mercy," we are changed.[11] Since all

human perfection consists in loving God, and since God's own love (in the form of his grace) is what leads the human person to God, it follows that God perfects us when we return his own love to him.[12]

## AN EXCHANGE OF LOVE

The idea that the human person could grow in grace through "re-gifting" his or her Maker fascinated C. S. Lewis. He observed in *Mere Christianity* that a father who gives his child sixpence so that the child may buy him a birthday present is ultimately sixpence none the richer.[13] Yet, Lewis added, once a man realizes that it is impossible for him to put God in his debt or to give God anything he does not already "in a sense" possess, God can then "really get to work."[14]

Later in life, Lewis offered further thoughts on how God works upon a person who is receptive to his gift of love. God communicates to the person a share of the "primal love" that comprises his "Divine energy"—that is, charity, which Lewis calls "Gift-love."[15] This Gift-love "desires what is simply best for the beloved."[16] It enables the one who receives it to make a complete self-offering to God.

Lewis writes with a palpable sense of wonder as he describes this self-offering, in a passage that recalls his sixpence analogy: "By a high paradox, God enables men to have a Gift-love towards Himself. There is of course a sense in which no one can give to God anything which is not already His; and if it is already His, what have you given? But since it is only too obvious that we can withhold ourselves, our wills and hearts, from God, we can in that sense, also give them. . . . 'Our wills are ours to make them Thine.'"[17]

Reading Lewis's words, I am drawn back to the words of the Suscipe. That prayer, in which I offer God "my entire liberty, my memory, my understanding and my whole will," is a perfect instrument for regifting God's own charity back to him.

A closer look at the Suscipe prayer can provide insight into the dynamic operation of grace upon the soul.

As we saw in chapter 1, Ignatius introduces the Suscipe in a section of his Spiritual Exercises called the Contemplation to Attain the Love of God. The saint begins his instructions for that contemplation with two preliminary observations: "The first is that love ought to manifest itself in deeds rather than in words. The second is that love consists in a mutual sharing of goods, for example, the lover gives and shares with the beloved what he possesses, or something of that which he has or is able to give; and vice versa, the beloved shares with the lover. . . . Thus, one always gives to the other."[18]

In highlighting love as a give-and-take, Ignatius is inviting the retreatant to undertake the contemplation with a heart full of gratitude.[19] He goes on to make this explicit, calling upon the retreatant to "ask [God] for an intimate knowledge of the many blessings" he or she has received, so that "filled with gratitude for all," the retreatant "may in all things love and serve the Divine Majesty."[20]

The contemplation is divided into four points, each beginning with a consideration of how God gives. God is contemplated as

1. the giver of creation, redemption, and all that the retreatant has personally received;

2. the giver of life to all creatures, of understanding to human beings, and of his own indwelling presence to the retreatant (who is created in God's image);

3. the giver of his own labor, working for the retreatant's benefit "in all creatures upon the face of the earth"; and

4. the giver of "all blessings and gifts," all of which "descend from above."[21]

In this way, Ignatius brings the retreatant to envision an ever-widening circle of thanksgiving, beginning with the personal and ending with the universal.

Francis, prior to his papacy, wrote to his fellow Jesuits that in this contemplation, "when St. Ignatius says that we should bring things to our memory, he is speaking about a retrieval of our history of grace. And the graces, given our sinful condition, are always gifts of mercy."[22]

And so it is that, within each of the exercises' points of contemplation, after reviewing his "history of grace," the retreatant enters into dialogue with the Father of mercies, praying the Suscipe: "Take, O Lord, and receive my entire liberty . . ."

The prayer in its original Latin begins, "Suscipe, Domine . . . ." Its first word comes from the verb *suscipio*, meaning to take up, catch up, support, or raise. A priest celebrating Mass in Ignatius's time would use the word *suscipe* during the offertory as he beseeched God to accept the wine and bread that he was to offer for consecration. In the same way, as Francis told his fellow Jesuits, when we pray our own Suscipe, "our devotion thus emerges from thanksgiving, from Eucharist. We are following Jesus to the place where he has made a complete act of thanks to the Father who is in heaven."[23]

So, from its very first word, we can detect in the Suscipe an upward motion. The prayer reflects the supplicant's desire that God elevate the love that he or she is offering—love that the supplicant first received from God himself—so that it may be acceptable to him.

In light of the Suscipe's upward motion, we can now see why it is so important to Ignatius that the prayer be prayed out of a deep sense of gratitude, for gratitude is the virtue that lifts up our heart. Francis tells us gratitude is "the response of love, made possible because in faith we are receptive to the experience of God's transforming love for us."[24]

Interestingly, another meaning of the verb *suscipio* is to take up a newborn child as one's own, "signifying the intention to rear it (instead of exposing it)."[25] This refers to an early Roman custom in which, according to one historian's account, "the father had the right of repudiating a newborn child. The child was placed at the feet of the father immediately after birth, and if instead of being lifted up by the father . . . , he was left on the ground, he was excluded from the *familia*."[26]

With that in mind, Ignatius's use of the word *suscipe* brings to mind the call of a son longing to be taken up into the arms of his heavenly Father. The image adds new meaning to St. Paul's emphatic teaching, "For those who are led by the Spirit of God are children of God. For you did not receive a spirit of slavery to fall back into fear, but you received a spirit of adoption, through which we cry, 'Abba, Father!'" (Rom 8:14–15; see also Galatians 4:6).

In the same way, we can see that, for Ignatius, surrendering our entire liberty does not mean consenting to be enslaved. Rather, it means submitting ourselves with complete humility to the Father's loving care, recognizing that, without his love, we are as vulnerable as a newborn exposed to the elements.

To what do we ask the Father to raise us? The prayer's next line hints at the answer as the supplicant offers up his memory, understanding, and will—the faculties through which, according to St. Augustine, the human mind is an image of the Trinity.[27] Ignatius's formula of self-offering seeks to elevate the retreatant into an ever-greater sharing in the love that flows from the Trinity's "eternal dialogue of communion."[28]

We can now understand why this particular contemplation comes to mind for Pope Francis in the interview where he describes his prayer as "always a prayer full of memory" (see chapter 1).

The opposite of memory is amnesia, which is, as theologian John Navone, S.J., observes, "an illness that involves an identity crisis"; its sufferers "forget their past, their story and their relationships."[29] But, Navone writes (in a book that is a favorite of Pope Francis), "Through faith, Christians share the same memories, the same history. Their sacred memories unite them as a people. . . . We share in the life of the Church, the people of God, if we share its memories."[30]

These memories, under the guidance of the Holy Spirit—whom the Father sends to teach and remind us (Jn 14:26)—enable us to hold fast to our identity in Christ. Francis affirms the connection between memory and Christian identity when, speaking of "the memory of God's works," he says, "It is this memory that makes me his son and that makes me a father, too."[31]

The Suscipe ends with the words, "Give me only your love and your grace; with these I will be rich enough, and will desire nothing more." With this request, the supplicant acknowledges Jesus' gentle admonition to Martha that "there is need of only one thing" (Lk 10:42): union with God in Christ.

## THE FREEDOM TO SURRENDER

When we make the loving self-offering of the Suscipe, and particularly in offering up memory, understanding, and will, we seek to be united to Jesus' own offering of love—the free choice he made to lay down his life for his friends: "No one takes [my life] from me, but I lay it down on my own. I have power to lay it down, and power to take it up again" (Jn 10:18).

And so, the "high paradox" described by Lewis—that in which God gives us the love with which we love him—comes about through the even greater paradox of our using our God-given freedom to make a perfect self-surrender to God. Satan said, "I will not serve," and is bound in chains, but the one who offers his entire self to the service of God in the company of Jesus enters into the freedom of divine life. In the words of Francis, "How beautiful it is to be able to face life's ups and downs in Jesus' company, to have his Person and his message with us! He does not take away autonomy or liberty; on the contrary, by fortifying our fragility, he permits us to be truly free, free to do good, strong to continue doing it, capable of forgiving, capable of asking for forgiveness. This is Jesus who accompanies us, the Lord is like this!"[32]

If gratitude is, as Francis says, "made possible because in faith we are receptive to the experience of God's transforming love for us,"[33] then a grateful heart is a receptive heart—one that is open to ever-greater transformation in Christ. For a model of such a heart, Francis points us to Augustine, who continually sought in prayer that his heart might be "full of God."[34]

Scripture tells us we do not have because we do not ask (Jas 4:2). Francis observes that Augustine received what he wanted—"a personal and profound relationship with Jesus"—because he asked for it. "It is a question of starting to say [yes] to Christ, and saying it often. It is impossible to desire it without asking for it. And if someone starts to ask for it, then he begins to change. Besides, if someone asks for it, it is because in the depths of his being he feels attracted, called, looked at, awaited. This is the experience of Augustine: there from the depths of my being, something attracts me toward Someone who looked for me first, is waiting for me first."[35]

Those words of Francis remind me of one of my favorite things about Augustine: the way he takes our human concept of unfulfilled desire and turns it on its head.

Unfulfilled desire is part of the human condition. As long as we are here on earth, subject to imperfection, illness, and death, we will want things that are beyond our capabilities (Rom 8:19–23). As the *Catechism* reminds us, only in heaven will we find "the ultimate end and fulfillment of the deepest human longings" (CCC 1024).

Augustine, while not disputing any of this, insists that our unfulfilled desires have a higher purpose. They help us loosen our heart's grip upon the good things that pass away, so that we might be able to open our heart to the good things that will endure forever. In Augustine's words, "Because now you are unable to see [God], let your task consist in desiring. The entire life of a good Christian is a holy desire."[36]

## "EMPTY WHAT MUST BE FILLED"

The classic scriptural example of a person unable to let go of earthly attachments is the rich young man who was unwilling to accept Jesus' invitation to follow him, because it would require selling his possessions and giving them to the poor (Mt 19:16–30; Mk 10:17–31; Lk

18:18–30). Pope Francis, preaching on Mark's account of the episode, says that the problem was that the young man's "restless heart," which the Holy Spirit was prompting "to draw near to Jesus and to follow him, was a heart that was full." Yet, "he did not have the courage to empty it"; instead, "he chose money."[37]

"His heart was imprisoned by it," the pope adds. "He was attached to money and he didn't have the freedom to choose." Therefore, in the end, "money chose for him."[38]

In painting a picture of a heart that is so full of money that it shuts out Jesus, Francis seems to be combining a pair of images that Augustine used in a homily to describe the human capacity for desire.

The first image Augustine uses is that of a small purse. Just as a small leather purse cannot hold a large amount of money unless it is stretched, so too, if we seek to be filled by God, our human desires need to be "stretched."

"What you desire," Augustine says, ". . . you don't yet see. But by desiring you are made large enough, so that, when there comes what you should see, you may be filled. For, if you wish to fill a purse, and you know how big what will be given you is, you stretch the purse."[39]

Augustine is speaking as one who knows what it is like to feel controlled by desire. As a youth, when he first began to feel the tug of grace upon his soul, he was so fearful of giving up his lustful way of life that the best prayer he could manage was, "Grant me chastity and continence, but not yet."[40] But as grace did its work, he found, to his surprise, that chastity was possible—not because he had ceased to desire but rather because his heart had become filled with a *holy* desire. That is why he could confidently tell his flock, "To the degree that a holy desire exercises us, we have cut off our desires from love of the world."[41]

To explain how we can put ourselves under the sway of a holy desire, Augustine turns to his second image: a jar filled with liquid. The key, he explains, is to "empty what must be filled."[42]

"You must be filled with the good," Augustine adds. "Pour out the bad. Consider that God wants to fill you with honey. If you are full of vinegar, where will you put the honey?"[43]

The image of being "full of vinegar" suggests a bitter heart, one that is clinging to resentment. Letting go, Augustine says, is painful but necessary: "What the vessel was carrying must be poured out; the vessel itself must be cleaned; it must be cleaned, even strenuously and by rubbing, so that it may become suitable for a particular thing." Cleansing our heart, we become suitable vessels for God.[44]

## RECONCILIATION AND "RE-CREATION"

One way to cleanse our heart is through the sacrament of Reconciliation. In *The Thrill of the Chaste* (Catholic edition), I share how the purifying effects of sacramental confession help me to overcome not only the darkness within but also the darkness without:

While it's no sin to be unhappy, the fact that there is any unhappiness in the world is due to sin. Whatever makes me unhappy is due to sins I commit, sins committed against me, or the general state of brokenness resulting from original sin.

The Sacrament of Reconciliation helps me deal with the effects of sin in all its facets. Where my own sins are concerned, sacramental confession does more than erase them. It leads me to examine where my sinful impulses are coming from and gives me the grace to fight those impulses when they reappear. When given a clearer awareness of those impulses and improved control over them, I can better deal with the pain of being sinned against, as well as the sad effects of original sin (human frailty, sickness, and death).[45]

Since writing those words and reflecting further on the role of sacramental confession in my own healing, I have been struck by a passage from Augustine that the *Catechism* quotes when discussing sacramental confession: "God created us without us: but he did not will to save us without us" (CCC 1847).

There is an alternate word that the Church sometimes uses to describe God's saving action in human souls, one that is a favorite of Francis. That word is *re-creation*—the mission of Jesus as he was reconciling the world in himself, in the name of the Father (2 Cor 5:19). "Everything else—healing, teaching, reprimands—are only signs of that deeper miracle which is the re-creation of the world.

Thus reconciliation is the re-creation of the world; and the most profound mission of Jesus is the redemption of all of us sinners."[46]

We could therefore, in a sense, rephrase Augustine's maxim and say that God created us without us, but he did not will to *re-create* us without us. He wills rather that we participate in our own re-creation. We do this through *reparation*—giving love to God and neighbor in return to God's love for us.[47] All the action of redemption is on the part of God; yet, in a mysterious but real way, he enables us to cooperate with him as he repairs the damage to our hearts that were broken by sin.

Pope Francis's encounter with Christ began in earnest on that spring day in 1953 when he sought re-creation in the confessional. Our own encounter with Christ likewise begins anew each time we seek God's mercy both for ourselves and for those who have harmed us. "In every act of charity," Francis says, "he re-creates his love within us."[48] With that in mind, let us make the prayer known as the Act of Charity, asking for the grace of renewal in Christ: "O my God, I love you above all things, with my whole heart and soul, because you are all-good and worthy of all love. I love my neighbor as myself for the love of you. I forgive all who have injured me, and ask pardon of all whom I have injured. Amen."

# 7

# AND I AM RICH ENOUGH AND ASK FOR NOTHING MORE

## *Sharing the Light of Christ*

||||||||||||||||||||||||||||||||||||||||||||||||||||||||||||||||||||||

Pope Francis can still recall the time he almost missed a train and caught an important life lesson.

It happened one day in the mid-1990s, during his tenure as an auxiliary bishop of Buenos Aires. Bishop Bergoglio was walking to catch a train to preach a retreat at a convent when he decided to make a detour to the cathedral so that he might pray before the Blessed Sacrament, as was his daily custom.

After spending a few minutes in prayer, Bergoglio was getting up to leave when a young man who appeared mentally unstable approached him asking to confess. The bishop gathered from the way the man slurred his words that "he was probably under the effect of some psychiatric medication."[1]

Recounting the interaction to his biographers, Bergoglio could not resist some self-deprecating humor: "So I, the witness of the Gospel, the one who practices apostleship, told him, 'Right now you'll just have to go to a father and confess to him, because I've got something to do.' . . . And I rushed out."

The bishop made it a few steps out of the cathedral before "a tremendous sense of shame" came over him as he thought about how the man would have to wait around until the priest came back on duty. He reentered the cathedral, heard the man's confession, and took him by the statue of the Virgin Mary to ask her to care for him. Finally he resumed his journey to the railway station, certain he had missed his train.

"But when I reached the station," Bergoglio recalled, "I discovered that service had been delayed and I could catch the same train."

Upon returning from the convent, before he even headed home, he sought out his confessor. "What I had done was weighing on me. I told myself, 'If I don't confess, I won't be able to celebrate Mass with this on my mind.'" He repented of the "attitude of superiority" that had caused him to think that it was more important for him to stay on top of his diocesan duties than to be available to a member of his flock who was hurting.

Bergoglio told this story as an example of what he meant by his trademark expression *transitar la paciencia*, "travel in patience." The phrase came to him as he was reading *A Theology of Failure*, by John Navone, S.J., which describes the patience of Christ.

"I did not travel in patience that afternoon in the cathedral, because I had to catch the train," Bergoglio explained, "but in the end I caught it anyway, because it was delayed. It was a sign from the Lord, who was telling me, 'See, I am the one who will sort out the story.'"

## PATIENCE, MATURITY, AND MEMORY

Francis understands patience as a boundary experience, enabling those who endure it to attain true maturity. As we saw in chapter 2, it is this kind of patience that he admired in his grandmother and in Peter Faber, who said, "Time is God's messenger."[2] He told his biographers:

> By reaching the limit, by confronting the limit, patience is forged. Sometimes life forces us not to ["do"] but to "suffer," enduring . . . our own limitations as well as the limitations of others.
>
> Traveling with patience is knowing that what matures is time. Traveling with patience is allowing time to rule and shape our lives. . . . [It] means accepting that life is a continuous learning experience. . . . To travel in patience is to make peace with time, and allow for others to open up your life for you.[3]

Since becoming pope, Francis has spoken about the role of patience in healing of memory. If patience fosters maturity, then it likewise enables us to come to terms with the pain of our past. We do this when we seek to understand our own memories in light of the memories of God, who remembers us. The words Francis speaks about this to the Church in general can be applied to each of us individually: "We must recover our memory, the memory of the Church that is the people of God. Today we lack a sense of history. . . . Everything is done in a hurry, because we are slaves of the moment. [We have to] recover our memory in the patience of God, who did not hurry his history of salvation, who has accompanied us throughout history, who preferred a long history for us, of many years, walking with us."[4]

If we find it difficult to appreciate how God has accompanied us, it is because we are seeing our history through our wounds. True healing begins, Francis says, when we seek to understand our history through *Jesus'* wounds. In a powerful meditation composed during his time in Buenos Aires, he asserts, "Our own flesh wounded by sin (the flesh of prodigal sons and daughters) is the entryway into the flesh wounded by love (the flesh of Jesus), which opens for us the way to the Father of all flesh. . . . By our wounds, through the Word made wound, we have access to the only One who is capable of embracing us in his mercy."[5]

The glorified wounds on Jesus' resurrected body are the fruit of his patient endurance. When we gaze upon them with the eyes of faith, we see the same tender patience with which God endured the complaints and sinfulness of his people throughout the times of the patriarchs and prophets. Jesus' Precious Blood reveals the invisible love of God that created us, sustained us, and brought us to this present time. "Through these wounds," Francis says,

> as in a light-filled opening, we can see the entire mystery of Christ and of God: his Passion, his earthly life, . . . his incarnation in the womb of Mary. And we can retrace the whole history of salvation: the prophecies— especially about the Servant of the Lord, the Psalms, the Law and the Covenant; to the liberation from Egypt, to the first Passover and to the blood of the slaughtered lambs; and again from the Patriarchs to Abraham, and then all the way back to Abel, whose blood cried out from the earth. All of this we can see in the wounds of Jesus, crucified and risen; with Mary, in her Magnificat, we can perceive that, "His mercy extends from generation to generation." (cf. Lk 1:50)[6]

# RECOVERY AND THE "HAPPY FAULT"

One of the formative influences upon my early years as a Catholic was a Jesuit named Francis who, like Pope Francis, had the courage to draw upon his own experience of woundedness in order to help others.

To his peers, Fr. Francis Canavan, S.J. (1917–2009), was a prominent Catholic intellectual and political theorist. Only his closest friends knew that, in addition to his many scholarly writings, he had also authored two slim volumes of spiritual reflections for his fellow recovering alcoholics, to whom he ministered as a longtime chaplain for the Calix Society (a fellowship group for Catholics who participate in Alcoholics Anonymous).

In one of those books, *By the Grace of God*, Canavan makes an observation that applies to my own experience, even though my woundedness was not caused by alcohol. He writes, "Alcoholism is a terrible disease to die of and a miserable one to live with. But it is a great disease to recover from."[7]

I love that statement, because one can fill in the blank with any disorder of the body, mind, or spirit, and it remains true. For me, PTSD is a miserable disease to live with. But it is truly a great disease to recover from—for, as Canavan goes on to say, recovery is more than living without the disease: "It also improves our attitude toward life as a whole, and teaches us how to live."[8]

The truth is that we gain something from recovery—something we might not have received, had we not been afflicted. It is, to use the language of the Church, a *felix culpa*, a "happy fault," because it opens the door to Christ's saving grace in our heart. "It gives us an understanding of God that gives our lives meaning and purpose. We begin to see what Our Lord, Jesus Christ, meant when he said to his disciples, 'If you continue in my word, you will know the truth, and the truth will make you free' (Jn 8:32)."[9]

Beyond the basic Christian meaning of Canavan's statement, there is also, I think, something about it that is profoundly Ignatian. I relate it to an observation made by the Jesuit spiritual author Joseph de Guibert, S.J., concerning the particular character of Ignatius of Loyola's spiritual gifts.

De Guibert writes that whereas some mystics receive spiritual gifts (infused graces from God) that primarily affect their intellect, and others receive ones that affect primarily their will, Ignatius was different. The Jesuit founder was the type of mystic in whom the infused gifts are not solely spiritual. "Instead, they affect both the spiritual and the bodily faculties, thereby including such powers as the memory and imagination which serve for execution. Thus these infused gifts themselves impel the mystic both toward union with God and toward service."[10]

We saw in chapter 1 that Ignatius suffered painful memories, some due to his own sinful thoughts and desires, and some due to trauma. And we also saw, in chapter 5, that Ignatius's imagination was wounded. Before his conversion, he was often preoccupied with worldly fantasies. With that in mind, what de Guibert is effectively saying is that the spiritual gifts Ignatius received were ones that enabled those *very same faculties that had been wounded* to "impel [him] both toward union with God and toward service."

Those last words from de Guibert remind me of the Twelfth Step of Alcoholics Anonymous: "Having had a spiritual awakening as the result of these Steps, we tried to carry this message to alcoholics, and to practice these principles in all our affairs."[11] "A spiritual awakening"—that is union with God. "To carry this message to alcoholics, and to practice these principles in all our affairs"—that is service.

Canavan found in his own life that the experience of recovery deepened his faith and strengthened him in his vocation. "If we have the gift of Christian faith," he wrote, "it is by a combination of God's revelation of himself, and our own experience. The Church teaches us what God has revealed about himself, but it becomes meaningful to us as it answers to, throws light on, and shapes our own experience. And it was a painful and humiliating one. But we can thank God for it, because it is the experience that made it possible for us to understand what God was trying to tell us all along."[12]

## THE WISDOM OF THE HEART

It may sound far-fetched to compare the spiritual awakening of an AA member to the outstanding mystical gifts that God granted to Ignatius. But even those of us who are not granted visions have access, through our Baptism and Confirmation, to the infused gifts of the Holy Spirit. Pope Francis, in a message for the World Day of the Sick, describes how one such gift can transform our sufferings into conduits of grace. It is the gift of wisdom, specifically the kind of wisdom known as *sapientia cordis*, wisdom of the heart.

"This wisdom," Francis says, "is no theoretical, abstract knowledge, the product of reasoning. . . . It is a *way of seeing things [that is] infused by the Holy Spirit* in the minds and the hearts of those who are sensitive to the sufferings of their brothers and sisters and who can see in them the image of God."

Importantly, the pope adds that our sufferings, accepted in faith, can have apostolic value regardless of whether we are capable of actively or consciously sharing our witness: "Even when illness, loneliness, and inability make it hard for us to reach out to others, the experience of suffering can become a privileged means of transmitting grace and a source for gaining and growing in *sapientia cordis*. . . . People immersed in the mystery of suffering and pain, when they accept these in faith, can themselves become living witnesses of a faith capable of embracing suffering, even without being able to understand its full meaning."[13]

The Christian witness of the sick—and of all who are wounded, whether their wounds are visible or invisible—is powerful precisely because, in their faith amid weakness and trial, they manifest "Christ the power of God and the wisdom of God" (1 Cor 1:24). In their lives, they provide ongoing testimony to the truth proclaimed by God through Jesus' resurrection.

This truth was the hope of Israel, as the Holy Spirit testified through a Jewish author during the century before Christ: "The souls of the righteous are in the hand of God, and no torment shall touch them" (Wis 3:1). It was also the hope of ancient sages such as Socrates, who, being condemned to die for his beliefs, told his judge and jury that a good man cannot be harmed either in life or in death.[14]

Jesus' resurrection proclaims this truth for all time—the truth that there is something more valuable than our earthly well-being. Pope Francis brings out this truth when he observes that Jesus, although having compassion upon the sick, healed them physically and spoke kind words to them so that he might point them to the highest form of healing: "There is something more important behind this. . . . These healings, these words that reach the heart are the sign and the beginning of salvation."[15] More important than that Jesus heals is that he *saves*.

## MEMORIES OF GOD, LOST AND FOUND

I remember, when I was a child of about five and learning about my Jewish faith at Sunday "Hebrew school," being puzzled at how, in stories from the book of Genesis and elsewhere in the Bible, man kept acting as though God did not exist. It was clear to me that man himself would not even exist if God had not created him and placed him in the Garden of Eden. How could he deny his Maker?

After all, I thought, from the time I was born, I had some idea who my father and my mother were. And Adam and Eve had even more cause to remember their Creator, because they, unlike me, were capable of reason from the moment they first opened their eyes in Eden.

How, then, could people in the days of Noah have been so wicked (Gn 6:5)? How could the people of

Babel have fixed their minds on building a tower up to the heavens, instead of loving the God who created heaven (Gn 11:3–4)? It made no sense to me. I was certain that if I were in their place, I would never have forgotten God.

But I did forget God. After I became a bat mitzvah at thirteen—showing I was a mature Jew by reading from the Torah during a Shabbat temple service—I fell away from faith. Rock music became my religion, and, despite being wounded by the effects of my childhood sexual abuse, I did not seek help from the Divine Physician. Instead, as I wrote in chapter 4, I sought love in things that were not love and became desperately unhappy. It was not until I was thirty-one that the light of Christ began to bring me out of the darkness.

While writing this book, I received an unexpected reminder of the time when I looked to rock and roll to elevate my soul. I was searching online media for reviews of my books when I happened across an item by a rock band, Los Negativos, from Barcelona, Spain. The band had posted a copy of an effusive fan letter I sent them in 1987, when I was eighteen.

I was astonished to discover Los Negativos's post, as I had never received a response to the letter and had assumed it never made it across the Atlantic.

Along with the image of my letter was a message from the band, written in Spanish. Not knowing the language, I used an online translation program to make out what it said. The group wrote that they had saved my missive because it was the best feedback they had ever received: "Wherever you are, dear Dawn Eden, a kiss."

My letter told of how I fell in love with Los Negativos's music after hearing a song of theirs that led me to purchase a copy of their debut album, *Piknik Caleidoscópico*. Given my limited teenage budget, the album had seemed like a high-risk investment, for I had never before spent money on music in an unfamiliar language.

"But," I wrote,

> once I listened to the album, I was surprised, because I usually like songs only when I can understand their lyrics. [Yet] even though I can barely understand a word of *Piknik Caleidoscopico*, your songs are so emotionally moving that I *feel* as though I understand them. . . . [It] is the best album I've bought this year. . . .
>
> How do I join your fan club? . . . Also, do you have any English translations of your lyric sheet available? I go around the house singing "tú ya sabes," and I don't even know what it means!

I smiled as I read that; I *still* didn't know what "tú ya sabes" meant.

Then I read down to the comments. One commenter had searched for my name and found to his surprise that I had become reborn as a Christian. "Los caminos del señor son inescrutables," he wrote.

I managed to grasp that even with my limited Spanish: the ways of the Lord are inscrutable. Indeed!

A band member responded to the commenter with the line from the song that I had sung to myself around the house, quoting the lyric in full. But after all these years, I still had no clue as to what it meant, so I resorted to the online translator.

What the translation said gave me goosebumps—but was it accurate? Wanting to be sure, I wrote to the band member to ask what the lyric meant, hoping his English would be better than my Spanish.

The band member, delighted to hear from me, quickly sent the answer: "The Lord said: You already know what I expect of you. You already know what I hope to receive from you."

Those were the words that I had sung to myself as a teenager, at a time when I was depressed, confused, and spiritually lost. I could not understand them, yet the sound of them set to music was so moving that I *felt* as though I understood them. So the Lord permitted me to sing: "Tú ya sabes lo que siento por tí, tú ya sabes lo que espero de tí . . ."

The words I sang came from the depths of my heart—a place so deep that only the Lord had access to it. They came from the part of my heart I had suppressed, the memory of my first love, before the evil of abuse and, later, my own sins had caused me to forget the Lord who made me. I already knew what he expected of me. I already knew what he hoped to receive from me.

I had forgotten God. But God had not forgotten me. He had put a song of love for him in my heart and on my lips—even though it would be years before I would be able to sing it with understanding.

## DARKNESS INTO LIGHT

Isn't it funny how the band whose songs had me unwittingly praising divine providence had a name that means "The Negatives"? Back when I was listening to Los Negativos, *I* was the one who was negative. My memory was consumed with the darkness of regret.

Although I became a Protestant Christian in 1999 and tried to get my life on track, it wasn't until I entered into full communion with the Catholic Church, seven years later, that I began to experience healing from the effects of PTSD. Receiving Jesus' Body in the Eucharist changed the way I lived in my own body.

Granted, grace doesn't destroy nature: as a Catholic, I continued to retain in memory the traumatic experiences that had caused me sadness and anxiety. But when, from time to time, some trigger would re-present the past pain to my mind and body, the experiences no longer affected me the way they had in the past. As I wrote earlier in this book, the effects of PTSD could still be painful, but they were no longer toxic. Instead, they were *purifying*.

How can this be? It is because the light of Christ has illuminated my "negatives"—all those memories of trauma and sin—and revealed them to be mere shadows. To be sure, the memories are of real events, but the effects of those events that remain in me have no real substance. They are like the sound of thunder that reaches us after the lightning has passed.

The words of Francis speak to my heart: "The incarnate Son of God did not remove illness and suffering from human experience but by taking them upon himself he transformed them and gave them new meaning. New meaning, because they no longer have the last word which, instead, is new and abundant life; transformed them, because in union with Christ they need no longer be negative but positive."[16]

Through the rays cast by Jesus' glorious wounds, I am able to see the past for what it is. It is a manifestation of the love of God, who awaited me and who, through his mercy, enabled all that I have done and suffered—even the painful and irreversible effects of sin—to work toward my salvation.

"The key," Francis has said, "is to understand the Cross as the seed of resurrection. Any attempt to cope with pain will bring partial results, if it is not based in transcendence. It is a gift to understand and fully live through pain. Even more: to live life fulfilled is a gift."[17]

Let us ask for the grace of understanding the Cross as the seed of resurrection, praying these words of Francis, through the merits of Christ's glorious wounds:

> Transfigure me, Lord, transfigure me,
> but not only me.
> Purify also
> all the children of your Father. . . .
> Transfigure us, Lord, transfigure us.[18]

# NOTES

||||||||||||||||||||||||||||||||||||||||||||||||||||||||||||||||||||||||||

## PREFACE

1. Gregory of Nazianzus, Epistle 101, quoted in "The Doctrine of the Atonement," in *The Catholic Encyclopedia* (New York: Robert Appleton, 1907), http://www.newadvent.org.

2. John Henry Newman, "Mental Sufferings of Our Lord in His Passion," in *Selections from the Prose and Poetry of John Henry Newman*, ed. Maurice Francis Egan (Boston: Houghton Mifflin, 1907), 151–52.

3. Ibid., 152.

4. Ibid.; italics in original.

5. Ibid., 153.

6. Antonio Spadaro, "Interview with Pope Francis," September 21, 2013, https://w2.vatican.va.

7. Francis, Encyclical Letter *Lumen fidei*, § 46.

## 1. RECEIVE, O LORD, ALL MY LIBERTY

1. Jorge Mario Bergoglio, "The Story of a Vocation," *L'Osservatore Romano*, January 3, 2014.

2. Sergio Rubin and Francesca Ambrogetti, *Pope Francis: His Life in His Own Words* (New York: Putnam, 2013), 23.

3. Ibid., 24.

4. Jorge Mario Bergoglio, *Open Mind, Faithful Heart* (New York: Crossroads, 2013), 214.

5. Rubin and Ambrogetti, *Pope Francis*, 24.

6. Ibid., 168.

7. Spadaro, "Interview with Pope Francis."

8. Ibid.

9. A novice is a person discerning religious life in the novitiate, which lasts two years, the first stage of Jesuit formation.

10. These details apply only to the Long Retreat, not to the Spiritual Exercises themselves, for it is not only Jesuit novices who make the exercises. In the exercises' nearly five hundred years of existence, they have been adapted for people in different states of life and of different faith backgrounds. They also may be given within a shorter period of time than thirty days.

11. The Church calls these events "mysteries" to emphasize that, while they took place in a certain historical time and place, they concern Jesus, who is both human and divine, and thus they can never be fully comprehended by the human mind. However much we may meditate upon them, there will always remain something mysterious about them, providing new matter for reflection.

12. Spadaro, "Interview with Pope Francis"; translation modified.

13. Ignatius of Loyola, *Spiritual Exercises*, § 53. All quotations from the *Spiritual Exercises* are taken from St. Ignatius of Loyola, *The Spiritual Exercises of St. Ignatius*, trans. Louis J. Puhl (Chicago: Loyola Press, 2010), http://spex.ignatianspirituality.com.

14. Spadaro, "Interview with Pope Francis."

15. Francis, "Meeting with Young People in Manila," Vatican Radio, January 18, 2015, http://en.radiovaticana.va.

16. Francis, "Vigil of Pentecost with the Ecclesial Movements," May 18, 2013, http://w2.vatican.va.

17. Jorge Mario Bergoglio, quoted in Silvina Premat, "The Attraction of the Cardinal," *Traces*, July 2001, http://archivio.traces-cl.com.

18. Bergoglio cites 1 John 4:19 when discussing the meaning of *primerea* in Rubin and Ambrogetti, *Pope Francis*, 41.

19. Francis Thompson, "The Hound of Heaven," in *Poems of Francis Thompson* (London: Continuum, 2001), 40.

20. Spadaro, "Interview with Pope Francis."

21. On the Mass as the great prayer that unites our individual prayers, see Pope Paul VI, Apostolic Constitution *Missale Romanum*, April 3, 1969, http://www.vatican.va.

22. Paul VI, *Mysterium fidei*, § 34, http://w2.vatican.va.

23. Francis, "General Audience," February 5, 2014, http://w2.vatican.va.

24. Ibid.

25. Francis, "General Audience," April 1, 2015, http://www.zenit.org.

26. At thirty-one, I had a dramatic conversion to Christianity and was baptized by a Protestant minister. Six years later, I was received into full communion with the Catholic Church. I share my conversion story in chapter 3 of *The Thrill of the Chaste: Finding Fulfillment While Keeping Your Clothes On*, Catholic ed. (Notre Dame, IN: Ave Maria Press, 2015).

27. I discuss my childhood wounds, and the healing I have received, in *My Peace I Give You: Healing Sexual Wounds with the Help of the Saints* (Notre Dame, IN: Ave Maria Press, 2012).

28. Translation and Hebrew transliteration (altered) from "Shabbat Evening Home Ritual," Judaism 101, accessed July 29, 2015, http://www.jewfaq.org.

29. Bergoglio, *Open Mind*, 251.

30. Ibid.

31. Francis, "Meeting with the Detainees," July 5, 2014, http://w2.vatican.va.

32. Jorge Mario Bergoglio, *In Him Alone Is Our Hope* (New York: Magnificat, 2013), 9.

33. Bergoglio, *Open Mind*, 251.

34. Jorge Mario Bergoglio, "Holding the Tensions," in "Writings on Jesuit Spirituality I," trans. and ed. Philip Endean, *Studies in the Spirituality of Jesuits* 45, no. 3 (Fall 2013): 26–27.

35. Bergoglio, *Open Mind*, 287.

36. Francis, "Papal Mass for the Possession of the Chair of the Bishop of Rome," April 7, 2013, http://w2.vatican.va.

37. Rubin and Ambrogetti, *Pope Francis*, 46.

38. Francis, "Papal Mass."

39. I also discuss the Suscipe in chapter 1 of *My Peace I Give You*, from which some of the material in this section is adapted.

40. Ignatius of Loyola, *A Pilgrim's Journey: The Autobiography of Ignatius of Loyola*, trans. Joseph Tylenda (San Francisco: Ignatius Press, 2001), 37.

41. Ignatius of Loyola, *Spiritual Exercises*, § 231.

42. Ibid., § 232.

43. Ibid., § 233.

44. Bergoglio, *Open Mind*, 101.

45. Bergoglio, *In Him Alone*, 125.

46. Francis, "Holy Mass on the Solemnity of Corpus Christi," June 19, 2014, http://w2.vatican.va.

47. Ibid.

48. Ibid.

49. Ibid.; italics in original, translation modified.

## 2. TAKE MY MEMORY, MY UNDERSTANDING, AND MY ENTIRE WILL

1. Brendan Comerford, "A Contemporary Pierre Favré? Jesuit Echoes in Pope Francis's Ministry of Consolation and Service," *Religious Life Review* (September/October 2014): 263.

2. Normally, for a holy person to be deemed "blessed"—the last step before canonization—the Vatican Congregation for the Causes of Saints has to verify that a miracle has taken place through his or her intercession. For the blessed to then be canonized, an additional miracle is required. The pope has the authority to bypass those rules at any time.

3. Brian O'Leary, "The Discernment of Spirits in the *Memoriale* of Blessed Peter Favre," *The Way*, supplement no. 35 (1979): 17.

4. Peter Faber, *Memoriale*, § 412. All quotations from the *Memoriale* are from Peter Faber, *The Spiritual Writings of Pierre Favre*, ed. Edmond C. Murphy and John W. Padberg (St. Louis: Institute of Jesuit Sources, 1996), 299.

5. At that time—the height of the Protestant Reformation—many European rulers were leaving the Catholic Church and commanding that their people do the same. Such defections weighed heavily on Faber, who, as a missionary, was on the front lines of the Church's battle to keep Europe from losing the faith. For him, rejection of the Church was rejection of Christ, as Jesus indicated when he spoke to a notorious persecutor of Christians (Acts 9:4): "Saul, Saul, why are you persecuting me?"

6. Murphy and Padberg, "Introduction," in *Spiritual Writings of Pierre Favre*, 25.

7. Faber, *Memoriale*, § 184.

8. Ibid., § 268.

9. Ibid., § 269.

10. Ibid., § 270.

11. Ibid.

12. Ibid., § 271.

13. Bergoglio, "Story of a Vocation with the Ecclesial Movements."

14. Francis, "Vigil of Pentecost with the Ecclesial Movements."

15. Spadaro, "Interview with Pope Francis."

16. Peter Faber, quoted in Francis, Apostolic Exhortation *Evangelii gaudium*, § 171, http://w2.vatican.va.

17. Faber, *Memoriale*, § 197.

18. Ibid.

19. Ignatius of Loyola, *Spiritual Exercises*, § 230.

20. Faber, *Memoriale*, § 198.

21. Ibid., § 203.

22. Ibid.

23. Ibid., § 103.

24. Francis, General Audience, February 12, 2014, http://w2.vatican.va.

25. Francis, "Homily at Holy Mass on the Solemnity of Corpus Christi," May 30, 2013, http://w2.vatican.va.

## 3. WHATSOEVER I HAVE OR HOLD, YOU HAVE GIVEN ME

1. Francis, "Address to the Camaldolese Benedictine Nuns," November 21, 2013, https://w2.vatican.va.

2. Ibid.

3. Francis, "Homily on the Solemnity of Pentecost," June 8, 2014, http://w2.vatican.va.

4. Ibid.

5. Francis, "Homily at Holy Mass on the 'Day of Catechists,'" http://w2.vatican.va.

6. Ibid.

7. Ibid.

8. Francis, "Message for the 22nd World Day of the Sick 2014," December 6, 2013, https://w2.vatican.va.

9. Geiger's observation and a few other reflections in this chapter are taken or adapted from chapter 2 of *My Peace I Give You.*

10. See, for example, Mark 10:33–34.

11. See Luke 19:11 and 24:21.

12. See Peter's rebuke to Jesus in Matthew 16:22.

13. See Luke 24:6–8. The homily I had in mind was Pope Francis's "Easter Vigil Homily," March 30, 2013, http://w2.vatican.va.

14. See Luke 24:13–35.

15. Francis, "Easter Vigil Homily."

16. "I am with you always, until the end of the age" (Mt 28:20).

17. Francis, Encyclical Letter *Lumen fidei*, § 40.

18. John Paul II, Encyclical Letter *Ecclesia de Eucharistia*, § 56, quoted in Jorge Mario Cardinal Bergoglio, "The Eucharist, Gift of God for the Life of the World," catechesis delivered at the International Eucharistic Congress, Quebec, Canada, June 18, 2008, http://www.vatican.va/. (I have translated the Latin word *oblationis* as "sacrificial offering"; the Vatican translation has "oblation.")

19. Francis, *Regina Coeli*, April 21, 2014, https://w2.vatican.va.

20. Francis, "Message for the 22nd World Day of the Sick 2014."

21. Francis, *Evangelii gaudium*, § 142.

22. Francis, "Easter Vigil Homily."

23. Francis, *Lumen fidei*, § 60.

## 4. I GIVE IT ALL BACK TO YOU

1. Patricia A. McEachern, *A Holy Life: St. Bernadette of Lourdes* (San Francisco: Ignatius Press, 2005), 68.

2. Daniel A. Lord, *Death Isn't Terrible* (St. Louis: The Queens Work, 1940), 15.

3. Francis, "Morning Meditation," June 9, 2014, http://w2.vatican.va.

4. Ibid.

5. Francis, *Lumen fidei*, § 37.

6. Francis, "Message for the 23rd World Day of the Sick 2015," December 3, 2014, http://w2.vatican.va.

7. Thomas Aquinas, *Summa Theologiae*, III, q. 73, a. 3, ad. 3 (Benziger Bros./Christian Classics translation).

8. Francis, "Lenten Message 2014," December 26, 2013, http://w2.vatican.va.

9. Ibid.

10. Ibid.

11. Francis, "Address to Participants in the 37th National Convocation of the Renewal in the Holy Spirit," June 1, 2014, http://w2.vatican.va.

12. "Pope's Q-and-A with Movements," May 21, 2013, Zenit, http://www.zenit.org.

13. Francis, *Lumen fidei*, § 31.

14. Francis, "Message for the 30th World Youth Day 2015," January 31, 2015, http://w2.vatican.va.

15. Ibid.; translation modified.

16. Augustine, *Homilies on the First Epistle of John*, 4.6. All quotations from Augustine's *Homilies on the First Epistle of John* are from Boniface Ramsey's translation (Hyde Park, NY: New City Press, 2008).

17. John Henry Newman, "Discourse 4: Purity and Love," National Institute for Newman Studies, 2007, http://www.newmanreader.org.

18. Francis, *Misericordiae Vultus* (Bull of Indiction for the Extraordinary Jubilee Year of Mercy), § 24, http://w2.vatican.va.

19. Francis, "General Audience," October 23, 2013, http://w2.vatican.va.

20. Ibid.

21. Francis, Encyclical Letter *Laudato Si*, § 241, http://w2.vatican.va.

22. Francis, "Message for the 29th World Youth Day 2014," January 21, 2014, http://w2.vatican.va.

## 5. AND SURRENDER IT WHOLLY TO BE GOVERNED BY YOUR WILL

1. Francis, "Morning Meditation," July 1, 2013, http://w2.vatican.va.

2. Francis, "Morning Meditation," October 10, 2013, http://w2.vatican.va.

3. Francis, "Morning Meditation," July 1, 2013.

4. Ignatius of Loyola, *Pilgrim's Journey*, 37.

5. Tylenda, "Introduction," in Ignatius of Loyola, *Pilgrim's Journey*, 15.

6. Ignatius of Loyola, *Pilgrim's Journey*, 42–43.

7. Ibid., 44.

8. Ibid., 45.

9. Ibid., 47.

10. Ibid., 48.

11. Ibid.

12. Ibid.

13. Ibid.

14. Spadaro, "Interview with Pope Francis."

15. George E. Ganss, ed., *Ignatius of Loyola: Spiritual Exercises and Selected Words* (Mahwah, NJ: Paulist Press, 1991), 377.

16. One prolific author on discernment who is faithful to the spirit and letter of Ignatius, and whose works come highly recommended by spiritual directors, is Timothy M. Gallagher, O.M.V., whose works include *The Discernment of Spirits: An Ignatian Guide for Everyday Living* (New York: Crossroad, 2005). A less thorough but more accessible treatment of the topic can be found in James Martin's *The Jesuit Guide to (Almost) Everything* (New York: HarperOne, 2012).

17. Ignatius, following traditional Catholic teaching, writes that there are three possible sources for our thought: God, the devil, or our own free will. See *Spiritual Exercises*, § 32.

18. "The enemy" is Ignatius's preferred term in the *Spiritual Exercises* for the devil.

19. Scrupulosity is treatable with the help of a good spiritual director. Since it is often, though not always, a symptom of obsessive-compulsive disorder, sufferers are also advised to seek help from a well-trained psychologist who respects their faith. The Redemptorists minister to those afflicted with scrupulosity through Scrupulous Anonymous, http://mission.liguori.org.

20. Ignatius of Loyola, *Spiritual Exercises*, § 350.

21. Ignatius of Loyola, *Pilgrim's Journey*, 70–71.

22. Viktor E. Frankl, *Man's Search for Meaning* (New York: Pocket Books, 1984), 147.

23. Ibid.

24. Ibid.

25. See Ignatius of Loyola, *Spiritual Exercises*, § 320–21.

26. Francis, "Morning Meditation," April 5, 2013, http://w2.vatican.va.

27. Ibid.

28. Jeffry Hendrix, *A Little Guide for Your Last Days* (Plano, TX: Bridegroom Press, 2009), 70–71.

29. Albert S. Rossi, "Saying the Jesus Prayer," St. Vladimir's Orthodox Theological Seminary, accessed July 31, 2015, http://www.svots.edu.

30. It is important to note that anyone who suffers self-destructive thoughts should seek professional help as well as the support of friends and family. During the episode I describe here, I sought and received psychological care, asked friends to pray for me, and spoke with my spiritual director.

31. Hendrix, *Little Guide*, 70–71.

32. Francis, "Morning Meditation," October 10, 2013.

33. Francis, "Meeting with Young People," January 18, 2015, http://w2.vatican.va.

34. "Collect for the Twenty-Seventh Week in Ordinary Time," in *Roman Missal*.

35. Francis, "Morning Meditation," October 10, 2013; translation modified.

36. Francis, "Morning Meditation," July 1, 2013.

37. Ibid.

## 6. GIVE ME ONLY YOUR LOVE AND YOUR GRACE

1. Francis, "Vigil of Pentecost with the Ecclesial Movements."

2. Rubin and Ambrogetti, *Pope Francis*, 40.

3. The Liturgy of the Hours (also known as the Divine Office) is also prayed by many members of religious orders as well as laity who wish to deepen their faith. It can be a powerful aid to healing of memory, as the one who prays it regularly becomes inserted ever more deeply into the liturgical rhythms of the Church.

4. Spadaro, "Interview with Pope Francis."

5. A more literal translation of the words is "by having mercy and by choosing."

6. Spadaro, "Interview with Pope Francis."

7. Francis, "Vigil of Pentecost with the Ecclesial Movements."

8. Jorge Mario Bergoglio, "Grant What You Command," 30 Giorni, December 2009, http://www.30giorni.it/.

9. Francis, *Lumen fidei*, § 36, 42.

10. Francis, "Morning Meditation," January 21, 2014, http://w2.vatican.va/.

11. Francis, *Lumen fidei*, § 42.

12. See Aquinas, *Summa Theologiae*, II–II, q. 184, a. 3 (regarding perfection in divine love); I–II, q. 110, a. 1 (regarding divine love in the form of grace leading people to God).

13. C. S. Lewis, *Mere Christianity* (New York: Scribner, 1952), 110.

14. Ibid.

15. C. S. Lewis, *The Four Loves* (New York: Harcourt Brace, 1991), 126, 128.

16. Ibid., 128.

17. Ibid., 128–29. The quotation Lewis gives at the end is from the Alfred, Lord Tennyson poem "In Memoriam A.H.H."

18. Ignatius of Loyola, *Spiritual Exercises*, § 230, 231.

19. Ibid., § 233.

20. Ibid.

21. Ibid., § 234–37.

22. Jorge Mario Bergoglio, "Holding the Tensions," *Studies in the Spirituality of Jesuits* (Winter 2013): 25.

23. Ibid., 27.

24. Francis, *Lumen fidei*, § 46.

25. Thomas Hewitt Key, *A Latin-English Dictionary Printed from the Unfinished Ms. of the Late Thomas Hewitt Key* (Cambridge: Cambridge University Press, 1888), 73.

26. William Smith, ed., *A Dictionary of Greek and Roman Antiquities* (London: John Murray, 1891), 352.

27. Augustine, *De Trinitate*, 10.11.

28. Francis, *Lumen fidei*, § 36.

29. John Navone, "God Reminds Us to Remember," *Homiletic and Pastoral Review* (May 2009): 56.

30. John Navone, *Triumph through Failure: A Theology of the Cross* (Eugene, OR: Wipf & Stock, 2014), 144. The book was originally published in 1974 as *A Theology of Failure*, which is the title under which Francis read it. See Jorge Mario Bergoglio, *Open Mind*, 297, where he acknowledges drawing from Navone's insights.

31. Spadaro, "Interview with Pope Francis."

32. Francis, "Meeting with the Young People of the Dioceses of Abruzzi and Molise," July 5, 2014, https://w2.vatican.va/.

33. Francis, *Lumen fidei*, § 46.

34. Augustine, "Exposition of Psalm 53," in *Expositions of the Psalms 51–72*, trans. Maria Boulding (Hyde Park, NY: New City Press, 2001).

35. Bergoglio, quoted in Premat, "Attraction of the Cardinal"; translation modified.

36. Augustine, *Homilies*, 4.6.

37. Francis, "Morning Meditation," March 3, 2014, http://w2.vatican.va.

38. Ibid.

39. Augustine, *Homilies*, 4.6.

40. Augustine, *Confessions*, VII.17, trans. F. J. Sheed (Indianapolis: Hackett, 2006).

41. Augustine, *Homilies*, 4.6.

42. Ibid.

43. Ibid.

44. Ibid.

45. Eden, *Thrill of the Chaste*, 33.

46. Francis, "Morning Meditation," July 4, 2013, http://w2.vatican.va.

47. This definition of reparation comes from the Apostleship of Prayer's "Recreation Document," December 3, 2014, which was approved by Pope Francis. See http://www.apostleshipofprayer.org/.

48. Francis, "Morning Meditation," September 9, 2013, http://w2.vatican.va.

## 7. AND I AM RICH ENOUGH AND ASK FOR NOTHING MORE

1. This story of Bergoglio's encounter with the man at the cathedral and what it taught the bishop about "traveling in patience" is

taken from Rubin and Ambrogetti, *Pope Francis*, 69–76; translation modified.

2. Peter Faber, quoted in Pope Francis, Apostolic Exhortation *Evangelii gaudium*, § 171.

3. Rubin and Ambrogetti, *Pope Francis*, 72–73.

4. Francis, "Address to Participants in Rome's Diocesan Conference," June 16, 2014, http://w2.vatican.va.

5. Bergoglio, *Open Mind*, 244, 246.

6. Francis, "Homily at Mass for the Faithful of the Armenian Rite," April 12, 2015, http://w2.vatican.va.

7. Francis Canavan, *By the Grace of God* (St. Paul, MN: Calix Society, 2002), 30.

8. Ibid.

9. Ibid.

10. Joseph de Guibert, *The Jesuits: Their Spiritual Doctrine and Practice* (St. Louis: Institute of Jesuit Sources, 1986), 55.

11. "The Twelve Steps of Alcoholics Anonymous," Alcoholics Anonymous, last updated June 2014, http://www.aa.org.

12. Francis Canavan, *The Light of Faith* (Minneapolis: International Calix Society, 2005), 6.

13. Francis, "Message of Pope Francis for the 23rd World Day of the Sick 2015," December 3, 2014, http://w2.vatican.va.

14. See Plato, *Apology*, § 41d.

15. Francis, "Morning Meditation," January 22, 2015, http://w2.vatican.va.

16. Francis, "Message of Pope Francis for the 22nd World Day of the Sick 2014."

17. Rubin and Ambrogetti, *Pope Francis*, 25.

18. Bergoglio, *Open Mind*, 125.